MW01505693

First-Century Youth Ministry
Exploring Our Jewish Roots to Reclaim Discipleship

By Heather Quiroz
Foreword by Mark DeVries and Jeff Dunn-Rankin

First-Century Youth Ministry

Copyright © 2020 by Heather Quiroz

Publisher: Mark Oestreicher
Managing Editor: Sarah Hauge
Cover Design: Adam McLane
Layout: Marilee Pankratz
Creative Director: Dag Felder

All rights reserved. No part of this book may be reproduced in any form by any electronic or mechanical means including photocopying, recording, or information storage and retrieval without permission in writing from the author.

All scripture quotations, unless otherwise indicated, are taken from the *Holy Bible,* New International Version, NIV. Copyright © 1973, 1978, 1984, 2011 by Biblica, Inc. Used by permission of Zondervan. All rights reserved worldwide. www.zondervan.com. The "NIV" and "New International Version" are trademarks registered in the United States Patent and Trademark offices by Biblica, Inc.

ISBN-13: 978-1-942145-50-9

The Youth Cartel, LLC
www.theyouthcartel.com
Email: info@theyouthcartel.com

Born in San Diego.
Printed worldwide.

Dedication

Jesus, you are the reason for my existence. You are my purpose in life. This book was birthed out of and because of my relationship with you. I pray that it honors you, gives you glory, and draws others closer to you. To my husband, Rodrigo, thank you for supporting me along this journey. Thank you for sitting with me and listening to me read chapter after chapter as you patiently offered words of encouragement and allowed me to process each one with you. I am so proud of you and of the man you have become in Christ. I can't wait to watch you grow as a father as you love, cherish, and protect our little girl, Adah. Adah, your mom loves you so much. I pray that as you grow, you fall in love with Rabbi Jesus, finding your worth, value, and identity in his love for you. Truly, that is my deepest desire for your life. To my parents, Charlie and Dawn, thank you for investing in me and showing me Jesus. To my sister, Andrea, and my brother, Christopher, thank you for your support in getting this project done. Both of you served me and for that, I am forever grateful.

Table of Contents

First-Century Youth Ministry

Foreword

With this provocative book, Heather Quiroz makes the case that the stories of the first-century church can (and should) shape the stories of today's church, particularly today's approach to youth ministry. As so many of us in youth ministry find ourselves in the spin cycle, trying our best to reinvent youth ministry with the latest, the newest, and the shiniest, we wonder: Is it possible that the innovative approach we're looking for was given to us 2,000 years ago?

Heather is suggesting a radical realignment of the ways we see youth ministry. Radical, as in starting at the root. And that root, Heather suggests, might just be found in our Jewish heritage—not just in the ways that Jesus led his disciples, but more interestingly, how a young, Jewish Jesus likely learned to follow God.

Everywhere we go, we meet youth workers who are tired of being in the business of program maintenance and behavior modification. They are longing to make disciples.

But the challenge to actually *make disciples* can easily get lost in the juggling act that is part and parcel of the profession of youth ministry. Though our context is worlds away from the one Jesus grew up in, is it possible to harvest from that world an approach to discipleship that goes beyond good theory to effective practice?

After working with over 1,000 churches to help them execute strategies that cultivate lifelong followers of Jesus, we can't miss the fact that the youth ministries that are thriving in America today are the ones that take discipleship seriously. Most youth aren't dying for another program to attend. They have plenty already. They are dying (sometimes literally) for a "rabbi" who will walk with them, live alongside them, and introduce them to a life worthy of their deepest affection.

"One of the biggest tragedies of our day," Heather writes, "is that we have incorporated God into our busy lives, instead of incorporating our lives into God."

Youth ministry leaders, for decades, have taught that programs must take a back seat to relationships. After his resurrection, Jesus didn't host a cutting-edge rally. He walked with friends and served them a meal. Of course, they experienced gut-wrenching disciple-making in the midst of it all, but the moments were centered around life together.

As Heather writes, "For Jesus and the culture that produced him, discipleship was a way of life. They did life together and incorporated every aspect of their lives into God."

Churches, of course, don't hire full-time youth pastors to "do life" with twelve young people. So maybe, though Heather doesn't say it directly, the model of first-century youth ministry is not meant to be done by those who get paid primarily for their job as professional youth ministers. Maybe the youth minister's job is also to cultivate a "community of rabbis" who together have the capacity to implement Heather's radical model.

The first century-model places Scripture front and center. The Bible isn't a seasoning. It's the meat and potatoes. The words of Scripture that Jesus learned as a child served as the soundtrack for his life and ministry. Heather suggests that a first-century ministry mindset puts the *Torah*—Scripture—at the center of the life, the teaching, and the culture we are seeking to create.

We know that in many contexts, memorizing Scripture can be seen as "so 1950s," but Heather is all about bringing it back. If a young teenage Jesus could memorize entire chapters and books of the Bible, is it crazy to think that our own teens could benefit from memorizing ancient truths that were designed to be a "lamp to my feet and a light to my path?" (We both happen to have at least that one verse memorized!)

Be forewarned. *First-Century Youth Ministry* raises the stakes for the youth worker. Like most innovative ideas, Heather's recommendations will increase the complexity before it is simplified. Elevating the work of discipleship while at the same time navigating church politics, managing required programs, and developing volunteer leaders will not simplify our work. But it may give us the kind of focus that that aligns all the disconnected pieces into a single, passionate vision.

To understand Heather's passion, it might help to know that she has been a take-the-hill athlete all her life. In fact, her epiphany came on a basketball road trip through Israel with Athletes in Action. So, when she confronts us with a question like, "How bad do you want it?" she's a player on the court, exhorting her teammates.

We first met Heather while we were leading a workshop at a youth conference. She leaned in, took notes, and asked a lot of questions. From time to time, she would summarize: "So I hear you saying …" Her summaries were so clear that we could see little light bulbs blink on for the other youth workers in the room. She was sort of the SparkNotes for that workshop. That very day, we invited her to join our Ministry Architects team.

You will notice immediately that Heather has done her homework for this book. Listening, studying, and asking the right questions. But she isn't offering this life-meddling advice from the safety of an academic classroom or a consultant's laptop. She is a passionate, boots-on-the-ground youth worker from the Midwest. This book is loaded with humble, endearing anecdotes about her own struggles while seeking to do ministry like the community that raised Jesus did.

We love that Heather has no qualms about rattling our cages a bit. Someone cared enough to turn her youth ministry life upside down in 2011, and she's willing to do the same for us.

If you want to keep doing normal youth ministry, put this book down.

If you're looking for a quick fix or a few hot ideas, look elsewhere.

If, however, you are longing for an approach to ministry that slakes your thirst for something deeper and more authentic—for your youth and for yourself—find a comfy chair and see if you don't hear the echoes of our Rabbi's voice in these pages.

Jeff Dunn-Rankin,
Executive Vice President, Ministry Architects
Mark DeVries,
Founder, Ministry Architects, Co-Founder, Ministry Incubators

Introduction

Not too long ago, a friend of mine who had a garden invited me to pick some of her lettuce because it was growing so fast that she couldn't use it all. She said to bring a pair of scissors so I could cut it for myself. When I got to the garden, there was a huge, beautiful, bright bed of lettuce. I started to cut off some, but it was taking longer than I had hoped, so instead of continuing to use the scissors I began to use my hands.

Using my hands made things go a lot faster, but the problem was that I started pulling out the roots. After a few seconds, it dawned on me: *Wait, if I pull out the roots, nothing more will grow!* I quickly stopped and later called my friend to apologize.

I have heard youth leaders across the country say it time and time again: "We've been doing discipleship all wrong. Students just aren't growing as disciples. We've got to do something different." I couldn't agree more! I've come to the realization that American evangelical church culture focuses more on programs than on people. As youth leaders, we are being challenged to ask ourselves some hard questions about how we've done discipleship. I think there's a better way, one found by unlocking our biblical heritage.

Is it possible that discipleship has been lacking in our culture because we inadvertently pulled up our Jewish roots? I believe we can find the answer to that question if we start to look back, asking God to reveal what lies underneath the surface of our faith.

If you've been plagued by a deep desire to see disciples made within your church setting, then this book is for you. It is for youth pastors, senior pastors, parents, youth leaders, and anyone else who cares deeply about guiding young people as they grow into disciples of the Lord Jesus Christ.

In these pages you'll learn a number of Hebrew words, gain a deeper understanding of Jewish practices—in particular, the Sabbath—and meet some great people like Billy, Katy, Zac, Ray, Lori, Cassidy, and two women named Jeanne! The interviews I conducted with these folks will help us see how discipleship can be applied in real life. The book will also provide practical tools to help you build a culture of discipleship in your youth program. Many of these concepts could even be applicable for a senior pastor hoping to deepen discipleship with adults.

This journey of exploring the Jewish roots of the Christian faith began for me in 2011 when I spent three and a half weeks in Israel on a discipleship tour with Athletes in Action (AIA), which is the sports ministry of parachurch organization Cru. AIA seeks to use sports as a vehicle to share the gospel across the United States and the world. Each morning of our discipleship tour, my fellow athletes and I would hop on a giant bus and explore Israel. It was awesome. We had no idea what each day would hold. We were asked to trust our teacher and trip leader, John, and go wherever he would take us. John is an expert in understanding Jewish life and culture from a biblical perspective. He's on staff with Athletes in Action and is also the founder of "Walk the Story," a ministry that takes individuals through Israel, visiting biblical sites as they watch God's story come to life. John's goal in leading these trips is to help participants understand what it might have been like to follow a rabbi as first-century disciples. During my short time in Israel, John taught me so much about faith that I hope to share with you in this book. You'll see me reference him quite a bit in my personal anecdotes.

After three and a half weeks in Israel I was deeply convicted that prior to this trip I had largely ignored the Old Testament. To my shame, I realized I had considered it just that: old. My experience gave me a renewed sense of love for the Old Testament and a passion to explore my faith's Jewish roots. This trip was the catalyst that sent me into a deep dive of study, reflection, and application. Once I returned home from Israel, I was so hungry to know more that I couldn't wait to get my hands on as much information as possible to keep growing in my understanding. Since then, I have read a number of books and listened to countless podcasts, videos, and teachings on first-century Jewish faith, life, and culture. I've had many conversations with friends who are experts in this area. I've also applied much of what I've learned within my youth ministry setting. All of my study has aided in shaping my philosophy of how I do youth ministry. I joke with my husband that I have a crush on Ray Vander Laan, the founder of That the World May Know Ministries, who is a true expert on the Jewish faith and culture of the first century and before. Through the study of all of this I feel like I've found a great treasure. I'm still exploring the depth and riches of what understanding the Jewish roots of the Christian faith can offer us in the twenty-first century.

As part of the trip, all of us participating played a two-week tournament on different basketball teams in either Bethlehem or Jerusalem. Between that and everything I was learning, plus the daily encouragement to reflect on and even experience some of what it might have been like to be a first-century disciple, that trip was unlike anything I've ever experienced. As we traveled throughout Israel under the hot desert sun, John would often ask us, "How bad do you want it? How bad do you want to be a disciple of Jesus? How bad do you want to follow him? How bad do you want to give up everything to make him known?" I'm going to ask you the same question. When it comes to the teens in your ministry growing as disciples, how bad do you want it? If you're desperate to see it happen, like I am, I promise that what you find here will motivate and encourage you to help make discipleship a reality for your ministry. If discipleship is already happening in your ministry, I believe you'll find some challenging ideas and useful tools to apply to your setting as well.

If we want to see real spiritual fruit in our youth ministry programs lived out in discipleship, we need to study the life and times of Jesus and the people he belonged to. We need to understand the people and biblical accounts that came before his time on earth. I'm hungry for teenagers and families everywhere to have a deeper walk with Jesus, to understand him more and live in greater obedience. Some of what you'll read in this book may feel alien, but as you read, ask God to help you understand your faith's Jewish roots and show you how to start applying this knowledge in small ways. After all, those Jewish roots nourished Jesus. Sometimes the best way to look forward is to look back, especially when things just aren't working.

I'm not trying to pretend that this book is going to fix all of your discipleship problems, but what I can promise is that if you journey through these chapters with me, you will be challenged and convicted. Make sure to strap on a good pair of sturdy sandals, because we're going on a walk with Rabbi Jesus (or as he's better known in Hebrew, *Yeshua*). We'll take a long, hard look at first-century Jewish life, culture, and practice to see just how he and his Jewish community did discipleship. You'll be encouraged to think about discipleship from a first-century perspective, you'll gain a greater understanding of the Jewishness of Jesus, and you'll be better able to start—or continue—instilling a culture of discipleship in your youth ministry setting.

Reclaiming Discipleship

I got lost in Israel by myself, a small, white female who only speaks English. I had to go by bus from where we were staying in Bethlehem to basketball practice in Jerusalem. Normally I wouldn't have traveled alone, but that night my teammate hadn't been able to join me for practice. John had told me to grab the first cab I could find to take me to the bus station, but I didn't listen to him. Acting like the overly frugal person I can be, I decided to save money on the cab and walk to the station. I have a pretty good sense of direction, and I thought I remembered how to get there, but somewhere along the way I took a wrong turn. Before I knew it I had no idea where I was. I was now wandering around the city of Bethlehem all alone and thinking the worst. It was awful, and I was scared half to death.

As the reality that I was lost set in, I started to panic. My mind raced with terrible things that could happen to me. *I'm going to get abducted, someone is going to rob me in broad daylight, my family will never see me again, all because I wanted to save ten dollars.* John was the expert on Middle Eastern culture, but I hadn't listened to what he told me to do because I thought I knew better.

Thankfully, I found a cab driver who understood enough English to get me to the bus station and my anxieties were relieved. During my short time wandering about the city of Bethlehem unsure of where I was going, I was deeply convicted of one thing: I need to listen and pay attention to the wisdom of those who have gone before me. In this context, that was John, a man who knew more about Middle Eastern culture—and geography—than me. A man whose past experiences had given him wisdom I now needed to apply to my situation.

In this book were going to do just that. We're going to explore what the Jewish roots of the Christian faith have to teach us about discipleship. We're going to see what we can learn from those who've gone before us and be challenged to apply what we've learned to our own ministry settings. In my experience growing up in the church and in my first few years of working as a youth pastor, no one ever encouraged me to look into my Jewish roots. However, once I started digging into them, I kept finding one treasure after another.

Doing Life Together

The heart of first-century Jewish life was not programs, but a commitment to what we might call "doing life together." This is a value many of us probably grew up appreciating. When I was a child my parents spent a tremendous amount of time with me. They were there with me through some of the most treasured moments of my life. I was loved enough for them to invest in me and help shape me into who I would become.

Each Christmas, my siblings and I would gather with Mom in the kitchen and bake cookies, fudge, and those weird pretzel sticks covered in white chocolate that tend to be the last things eaten on the Christmas cookie plate. Then, we'd prepare around twenty or so heaping plates to give to family and friends. My mom's giving attitude taught me how to share what I had with others. Meanwhile, my father spent more hours with me on the softball diamond than I can count. He had a passion for sports, and I followed in his footsteps. Through our time on the field together, my father taught me about hard work, dedication, and how to be a team player. It was in these times of "doing life together" that I learned the most from my parents.

Could it be that things like Christmas cookies and softball are the keys to unlocking what discipleship is supposed to look like? Could it really be that simple? I think so. Unbeknownst to my parents, they were instinctively doing something we see demonstrated in the life of Jesus. Jesus's "doing life together" model of discipleship was deeply rooted in Jewish life, culture, and practice. At the heart of Jewish life was a strong focus on community. This is hard for us to grasp as Westerners because we're so focused on our own independence, or sometimes on the lives and needs of our immediate family, that we don't quite understand what community is really supposed to look like, especially in the church. What would happen if we stopped just doing church and started doing life together?

A Journey with Rabbi Jesus

When I traveled to Israel in 2011, I had been working in youth ministry for a few years at a church in Illinois. At that point I had very little love for the Old Testament. Also at that time, my ministry and time weren't spent on investing in relationships, but instead were focused on numerical growth. I hardly knew the teenagers in my youth ministry, and much of my time was spent pursuing my own success rather than on building meaningful relationships centered on discipleship. Sadly, I also didn't spend much time studying God's Word or have a deep desire to know it in a real, life-changing way.

My world was quickly turned upside down upon arriving in Israel. My fellow participants and I opened the Scriptures together, hiked many, many miles, and were challenged to start seeing the Bible through the eyes of a first-century Jew. I couldn't believe what I was learning. I had grown up in church all my life, but our director's teaching was opening my eyes to see the Bible in a way I never had before. I wasn't just studying at home or sitting in a class, I was experiencing the Bible and watching it come to life. Something in my heart sprang to life during our three and a half weeks there: a desire to know and understand the Jewishness of Jesus. I felt a longing to understand what life and culture were like prior to and during the first century. In Israel, I fell in love with the Old Testament as I started to see it through Middle-Eastern eyes.

I returned home beaming with excitement over the things I had learned, which I couldn't wait to share with others. What I had experienced in Israel left a mark on my heart and mind that I still can't shake. There is something about Rabbi Jesus I experienced there that, I believe, is the key to unlocking what true, lasting, life-giving discipleship can and should look like within our youth ministries. I call it "First-Century Youth Ministry."

Sometimes I think we're a bit uncomfortable embracing our Jewish roots and seeing Jesus as a first-century Jewish rabbi. I'm not alone in this thought. In *Our Father Abraham*, Dr. Marv Wilson writes that

> ...many Jewish Christians seem to have little knowledge about their biblical roots. They have never really penetrated the inner world of biblical thought. Christians can converse intelligently about the latest automobiles, fashions, music, and sports, but too few give evidence of a deep understanding of their spiritual heritage. At best, their grounding in biblical soil is both shallow and shaky. Hence, they usually embrace an uncritical conformity to the prevailing spirit of today's world.[1]

Furthermore, as Wilson adds,

> After all, Jesus was a Jew, not a Christian of Gentile origin. His teachings, like those of his followers, reflect a distinct ethnicity and culture. The evidence found in the New Testament is abundantly clear: as a mother gives birth to and nourishes a child, so Hebrew culture and language gave birth to and nourished Christianity.[2]

Due to our own limited understanding, we have tried to view the Bible through a Westernized perspective instead of a Middle-Eastern one. We have unintentionally stripped off its Jewish roots because we are not quite sure what to do with them. Until we truly contextualize Jesus and his message, we will misunderstand much of what he said.

Understanding Your Roots

My paternal grandfather died when my dad was young. My dad's mother, my grandma Lily, died when I was only six. I remember elements of her life—her love of purple, her homemade egg noodles—but my memory of her is at best fragmentary. My maternal grandparents are still living. They are tremendous people and I'm thankful that to this day I have the opportunity to learn from them. I understand who my mom has become and who I've become due in large part to what I see in her parents. I lack this close, personal knowledge of my dad's side of the family, and because of that, I am less clear on how my dad came to be who he is.

In the same way that I have questions about how my dad came to be my dad as I know him, I wonder how we can fully know Jesus, and ourselves, without knowing our ancestral history. And beyond that, is it possible to understand what discipleship can look like in our youth ministry settings without having a grasp of the Jewish idea of community in the first century, or a sense of the time commitment it took to be a disciple who followed a rabbi, or an understanding of the relationships between important Old Testament figures like Elijah and Elisha? Just as spending time with my maternal grandparents led to understanding my mom, spending time with biblical greats, as well as gaining an understanding of the culture and practices of the Jewish people of the Near East, will increase our understanding of Jesus.

Prioritizing Discipleship

As I mentioned, when I first started out in youth ministry, my ministry was more focused on things like gathering a big crowd and pulling off an exciting outreach event than doing the hard work of investing in people and making disciples. Let's be honest, many of us become easily enthralled by youth pastors with big numbers. We wonder what *their* strategy is—instead of looking at the Scriptures to find what strategy Jesus used. We spend more time coming up with a flashy game to play than we do studying the Scriptures.

In the past, my discipleship priority list looked something like this:

- Have a small group tacked onto the end of youth group for twenty to thirty minutes, because I needed at least the same amount of time to give my message. (Because, in my own mind, my thirty-minute message was really important, mostly for the stroking of my own ego).
- Serve at a soup kitchen once or twice a year.
- Go on a weeklong mission trip once a year (then watch as everyone goes back to normal life).
- Put together some really big outreach events and gather a large crowd.

Perhaps you've had some of the same things on your list. This is a very Westernized way of thinking about youth ministry. It's difficult for us to operate outside of what we've always known, or to even consider that another way of doing things could actually work. It's kind of like when my husband and I argue over what being "on time" means. Rodrigo grew up in a Hispanic culture where being "late" was completely acceptable and no one was offended by it. Having been raised in American culture, I have been conditioned into believing that being late is offensive. When working with my husband's family, however, I have to let go of my Anglo conception of time and see things their way. In a similar sense, if we want to be able to see youth ministry differently, we have to remove our Westernized glasses and put on a pair of Middle-Eastern glasses. When we do, we'll see Jesus, and our youth ministry, in ways we never have before.

I think we often fail to realize that Jesus understood youth ministry. Have you ever sat back and reflected on the reality that (though it looked a bit different because of his culture and context) Jesus had a youth group? His was made up of eleven young men and one slightly impulsive adult leader in Peter. (I'll unpack the age of the disciples in the chapters to come.) That's right—he invested his life in a small group of young people, and those young people carried on in their faith, bringing about spiritual multiplication that changed the world.

Taking an Honest Look

Community was at the center of Jewish life, which revolved around Sabbath-keeping, family, and doing life together to grow the community in love, support, and deeper relationships.[3] In our Western world, life tends to revolve around our own vain attempts at success, our busyness, having a successful career or ministry, and becoming someone "important."

Sometimes it's hard for me to be taught by others because I want to be the teacher. This is fairly common in our culture: to want to be the strongest, brightest, and most important person. One of the reasons it's difficult, or doesn't even occur to us Westerners, to look at the history of our faith is that to do so we have to set aside so much of what we've learned or assumed and be students, accepting things that defy what we've previously believed. This is often a great lesson in humility.

The greatest harvest of fruit in the disciples' lives was after Jesus's resurrection as they began applying what he taught them. Unfortunately, since some of our egos are tied up in our ministries, we often have a hard time investing in people regardless of whether we see immediate results. There is a seductive sense of safety in the job security that large numbers give us. I wonder how many churches in the Western world would fire Jesus if he were their youth pastor? Probably more than we'd care to admit.

It's Not About a Program

So, what's going to be different about the model I suggest? I think you will see that it's fundamentally rooted in how God has wired us as people. As you read, you'll see that first-century discipleship is not centered around creating a cutting-edge program, it's all about learning to do life together. For Jesus and the culture that produced him, discipleship was a way of life. They did life together and incorporated every aspect of their lives into God. One of the biggest tragedies of our day is that we have incorporated God into our busy lives, instead of incorporating our lives into God.

I find it interesting that 2,000 years after the death and resurrection of Jesus, the writers of *Growing Young*, who studied over 250 church congregations with thriving ministries to teenagers and young adults, have targeted these six essential strategies for reaching this generation of young people:

1. Unlock keychain leadership. Instead of centralizing authority, empower others— especially young people.

2. Empathize with today's young people. Instead of judging or criticizing, step into the shoes of this generation.

3. Take Jesus's message seriously. Instead of asserting formulaic gospel claims, welcome young people into a Jesus-centered way of life.

4. Fuel a warm community. Instead of focusing on cool worship or programs, aim for warm peer and intergenerational friendships.

5. Prioritize young people (and families) everywhere. Instead of giving lip service to how much young people matter, look for creative ways to tangibly support, resource, and involve them in all facets of your congregation.

6. Be the best neighbors. Instead of condemning the world outside your walls, enable young people to neighbor well locally and globally.[4]

All of these strategic methods for keeping our young people engaged in the church are found at the heart of Jesus's ministry and teaching on discipleship. It seems to me that voices in the youth ministry community are already calling us back to the basics of what Jesus taught during the first century. As our eyes are being opened, we're recognizing that a total shift must to take place in order for us to start truly making disciples in the way Jesus taught us to.

Here is a first-century checklist for discipleship:

1. The Torah (the first five books of the Bible) was at the center of life, teaching, and culture.

2. The community, not the individual, was the primary focus.

3. To follow a rabbi meant something radical: It meant that you wanted to be just like the rabbi, in every way possible.

4. A rabbi was someone whose life was worth following because of how they loved God and his Word.

5. Discipleship was not a program; it was about learning and doing life together.

6. Mentoring was deeply rooted in the Scriptures and mentoring was how ministry was passed on from one individual to another.

Now, let's contrast this with a similar list of what many modern-day youth ministries look like:

1. Fun/pleasing parents/having a happy elder board is at the center of life, teaching, and culture.

2. The individual and their preferences are the primary focus.

3. To follow Jesus is more about having a friendship with him, based on your feelings, than it is about letting go of everything to take up a brand-new life.

4. A youth pastor is someone who is cool and attractive to teenagers, not necessarily someone who is a good teacher and passionate about God's Word.

5. Discipleship is a program and numbers are the indicators of success and growth.

6. There's not much time for real mentoring, because we're busy running outreach events and other big programs.

Our teenagers need and deserve so much more than just a program. Referring to conclusions from his research, pastor and author Chap Clark writes,

> As I studied students and culture, I came to believe that we as a society have allowed the institutions and systems originally designed to nurture children and adolescents to lose their missional mandate. In other words, society has systemically abandoned the young.[5]

Clark calls the youth ministry community to engage once more with young people on a deep, trusting, relational level. There are many, many teenagers who come through our doors each week who feel deeply alone, unseen, and unknown. I sometimes felt this way as a teenager, and the people who meant the most to me during that time in my life were the ones who simply took a minute to ask, "Hey, how are you? Is everything okay?"

I distinctly remember a softball coach who genuinely cared about me. Although he wanted me to become a better athlete, I could tell that he was more concerned with my well-being. I'll never forget a pitching lesson that was cut short when my coach pulled me aside and said, "Heather, I'm concerned about you. Is everything okay?" Then, after listening, he offered some helpful and encouraging words. Little did he know that my young teenage heart was about to burst at the seams with so much pent-up pain it was overwhelming. His gesture was so simple, but it made a major impact on my sixteen-year-old self.

Teenagers need to know that we care more about them than our programs. As Clark writes,

> By the time children, even the successful ones, reach high school and middle adolescence, they are aware of the fact that for most of their lives they have been pushed, prodded, and molded to become a person whose value rests in his or her ability to serve someone else's agenda.[6]

Could it be that our youth ministries are not actually serving our teenagers, but instead our own agendas? To me, it's terrifying to contemplate that our youth ministry programming is quite possibly not helping the problem but exacerbating it. It's imperative that we as youth leaders return to "doing life together" the way Jesus did in his discipleship if we truly want to meet teenagers' actual needs. That is why, my friend, we must no longer be okay with how we've done discipleship. For the sake of those lonely teenagers in our midst who constantly feel like they are serving one more adult's agenda, something has to change.

Here's some good news, though: We are not called to do this thing alone. Jesus understood this. Although he was the primary leader of his ragtag group of young people, he understood that eventually he would go to the cross and that his time of leading the charge on this earth would come to an end. Jesus had a plan from the beginning to train up, invest in, and employ the next generation of leaders. He went to the outcasts and the school dropouts (we'll look at this more in the chapters to come) and made them feel loved, valued, and encouraged, and he enabled them to take up the torch of making disciples after he left this earth. We need to follow his example. We can no longer use the excuse that people just don't want to serve in youth ministry, or that we just can't find good volunteers. Instead, we must go to people, showing that we believe in them, valuing what they have to offer, and investing everything we have in them as we raise them up as leaders. Because of our investment in them, these leaders will also know how to disciple, encourage, and train up young people. In essence, this is how Jesus did discipleship. When we follow his lead, we are no longer simply youth pastors who run good programs. We are disciple-makers who invest in people, just like our Rabbi Jesus.

A Treasure to Behold

I was immensely challenged back in 2011. As our group sat together for the first time at the gates to one of Solomon's courtyards, I felt like everything in my entire world had been turned upside down. When it was time to go home I didn't want the journey to end. With the new perspective I'd gained, in many ways, the first twenty-six years of my life in the church now felt a little bit like a lie. I don't recall learning about Jesus from his first-century Jewish context as a child and because of that there were deep and glorious biblical truths that I had never even heard about until my feet hit the dusty soil of the land of Israel. "Why didn't someone tell me this before?" I wondered many times. I had to learn to not become disappointed or upset with my church upbringing, but instead to have grace and compassion for the very fact that my experience in all of this, I'm sure, is not unique. I know this to be true because once I arrived back in the United States, people were surprised and blown away by some of the things I shared with them. Returning home in many ways felt like stepping off of a spaceship and back onto planet earth—a place where people didn't get me, because they hadn't been on the journey I had, watching God's Word come to life. They had never learned about the Jewish culture and practices that surrounded Jesus's life, either.

I'd learned so much about Jesus and the historical context of Christianity that I'd never realized before. The truth is, I know none of this was purposeful: we just, collectively, lost sight of the Jewishness of Jesus. And now we've got to get back to understanding him. As Dr. Cheryl Hauer writes in her article "Discipleship and the Hebraic Worldview,"

> *Yeshua* was Jewish. He was raised in an observant Jewish home by parents, who followed Jewish law and tradition; He lived in a Jewish homeland called Israel and spoke its language, Hebrew. He was a part of a robust and lively community that was identified by its active relationship with the God of Abraham, Isaac, and Jacob. He started life as all Jewish baby boys would— circumcised on the eighth day.[7]

We Cannot Change Who Jesus Is

There are moments when I want to make my husband like me. I want him to see the world more like I do—and therefore less through the lens of the Hispanic culture he was raised in. But I've learned that trying to fit my husband into the mold I'm attempting to create for him not only doesn't work, it actually hurts our relationship. When I finally surrendered my foolish desires to mold my husband into the person I thought he should be, our marriage started to flourish and I began to have a deeper appreciation for our cultural differences.

Jesus doesn't want to be squeezed into our own little boxes either. He wants us to know him fully, and in order to do that, we must embrace him as he is. Not only will our relationship with him flourish as we do this, but our appreciation for the culture in which he was produced will too.

Transformed by the Torah

One of the most powerful moments I had in Israel wasn't on the day we spent hiking up the Southern Steps, bounding up the same stairs Jesus would have used to get to the temple. Nor was it on the day we climbed Mount Carmel, envisioning Elijah calling down fire from heaven to consume the sacrifices of Baal. No, it was when I witnessed a young Jewish teenager do something that literally made me stop dead in my tracks, my feet frozen to the ground in wonder and amazement.

It happened the day we spent inside the city of Jerusalem. Jerusalem is a busy, bustling hub of religious life and culture. Inside the city walls our group came across a Jewish teenager standing in front of a podium with a very large book open in front of him. He was wearing traditional Jewish religious accoutrements, surrounded by family, friends, and mentors. Speaking in Hebrew with his eyes closed, his finger was running across the book sitting on the podium.

Intrigued by the scene before me, I asked John, "What is he doing?"

"This is the day of his bar mitzvah," John explained. "He's quoting a number of chapters from the Torah by memory. Historically, some Jewish boys even have the entire Torah memorized."

"Wait, what? A thirteen-year-old can do that?!" I was stunned. Not just single verses—whole entire chapters! And some may even know the first five books of the Bible?! The rest of my group continued on, but I felt as though time stood still for me. I pondered what I had just witnessed and the implications for my ministry setting. I was challenged and humbled to my soul.

I thought to myself, *Do the students in my ministry have very much Scripture memorized? Do I even have much Scripture memorized?* Sadly, the answer to both of those questions was no. When I went home I made a commitment to myself to start becoming a student of the Word. I recognized my sense of conviction about this in the words of Rabbi Abraham Joshua Heschel that are included within Wilson's *Our Father Abraham*: "what we need more than anything is not textbooks but text-people. It is the personality of the teacher which is the text that the pupils read; the text they will never forget."[1] I want to be that kind of woman. One who is so saturated in God's Word that it leaps from my heart and into the lives of everyone I meet. In order for this this to happen, something had to radically change in me.

Devotion to the Torah

I kept thinking, *What if the teenagers in my ministry knew the Scriptures like this young man does?* Now, I understand that Scripture memorization doesn't always equate with spiritual devotion. However, the Word of God is living and active (Hebrews 4:12) and it serves as a light unto our feet (Psalm 119:105). David said he hides it in his heart so that he might not sin against God (Psalm 119:11). Jesus is the Word made flesh (John 1:1). Since he is the Word, knowing his Word will help us better know and understand our Savior.

That day in Israel forever changed how I personally studied Scripture, and it changed how I taught it to others. A fire was lit inside my soul, ignited by the devotion of one teenager. Little did he know, God used him and his devotion to reshape my study and dedication to God's Word.

The Torah, the first five books of the Bible, is at the center of Jewish life. To a Jewish person, the Torah is the revelation of God. (To the Christian, Christ is the revelation of the Torah.) Devout Jewish people value the Torah so much that they recite it daily, seeking to put it into practice. In addition, each day and evening, devout Jewish families also recite the Hebrew Shema, which is Deuteronomy 6:4-5: "Hear, O Israel: The LORD our God, the LORD is one. Love the LORD your God with all your heart and with all your soul and with all your strength." This simple Scripture is something many Jews cherish with all their being. It reminds them of who they serve and how they are to live. I am convinced that it would benefit us in the youth ministry community to adopt a similar love, devotion, and passion for God's Word.

A Shema Failure

Not long ago, a Messianic Jew came as a visiting speaker to my congregation. This gentleman explained that his family recited the Hebrew Shema daily. I went up to talk to him after church. "When I was in Israel, we would say the Shema in Hebrew each morning," I said. "Can I recite it to you now to see if I still remember it?" He looked at me, quickly turned to his four-year-old son, and said to him, "I want you to listen to her to see if she knows the Shema." I crouched down to get myself face-to-face with this young Jewish boy and started to recite it.

As I began speaking the words of the Shema, this young boy's face beamed with joy and excitement. However, his smile soon turned to a frown when I stumbled with my Hebrew, probably starting to sound like Charlie Brown's teacher. I knew the sour look on his face meant I had said something wrong. "How did I do?" I asked once I'd finished. Without hesitation he shook his head in disgust, looking at me as if I'd told him we were having BLT sandwiches for dinner.

Young Jewish boys and girls would have spent many hours studying and memorizing and reciting the Torah. There are a number of practices that help with memorization. One method that aids young boys and girls as they memorize Jewish prayers is called *davening*, which is swaying back and forth during the recitation of those prayers.[2] In my travels I witnessed many young girls davening near the Western Wall in Jerusalem, holding the Torah close to their hearts as they swayed, reciting the Jewish prayers. Lois Tverberg met a rabbi in Israel who helped explain davening to her:

> The rocking motion during prayer, I discovered, is a way of expressing that one's whole self, body and soul, is caught up with God. The old rabbi explained that the movement of the body mimics the flickering flame of a candle, calling to mind the saying that "the candlestick of God is the soul of a man."[3]

I was blown away by the devotion of the young women I witnessed. Their passion for memorization was palpable. Their body language and posture showed radical love and dedication to memorization that inspired and challenged me. As they spoke the Jewish prayers, swaying rhythmically back and forth, it was as if their very lives depended upon the words they were speaking to God.

Davening is simply a tool for memorization, but this practice demonstrates something very powerful. When I witnessed it in Israel, I saw the hearts of those who held the Torah close to their hearts, swaying rhythmically back and forth, reciting the Jewish prayers with true commitment and radical devotion.

The Highest Form of Worship

Devout Jewish people in the time of Jesus understood the study of the Scriptures to be the highest form of worship.[4] Their sages believed that their study and devotion were what brought them closest to God. As Dr. John Garr writes in his article "Lamed—The Tallest Letter,"

> The words for worship both in Hebrew (*segad*) and Greek (*proskunéo*) mean to "prostrate oneself in the presence of the Deity." The ultimate form of prostration before God— submission to His will—is demonstrated in the study of the Scriptures with a view toward doing what God has said.[5]

What About You?

What about us? Do we have this same type of devotion to and reverence for God's Word? Do we study it and memorize it as part of our daily practice? I don't know about you, but there were weeks for me as a youth worker where I would spend more time preparing for the group game than studying Scripture for my lesson.

If we're hoping to create an atmosphere where the Word of God is a high priority in our youth ministries, here are some things to consider:

1. Start them young. Try having a conversation with your children's ministry leader about creating a plan to incorporate memorizing Scripture into the ministry.

2. Get parents on board. We all know that whatever we teach only goes so far. Without parents on board, it's difficult to get things in motion. Try meeting with parents to share your vision for God's Word and ask them to join you in it.

3. Challenge your teens. While mentoring a teenager, try memorizing some verses or an entire book of the Bible together, with the goal of reciting those Scriptures or that entire book to your youth ministry at some point. Make memorization and recitation part of your weekly events.

4. Start with yourself. A lot of what you share with teenagers comes from your own personal devotion to God. If your devotional life is lacking, try making your time in God's Word a greater priority. You and your teens will benefit from it.

5. Study the books of the Bible in full. Instead of going through a topical series, try walking through a book of the Bible with your group. This creates synergy as you study God's Word and offers you an opportunity to unfold God's story in a more interconnected way, focusing on the characters, history, culture, and context of the Bible.

Taste and See

Jesus himself would have had not only the entire Torah memorized, but the books of the prophets and wisdom literature as well. This was common for the sages of Jesus's day. Spending time in the Word of God was a daily practice. The Talmud (the authoritative body of Jewish tradition, comprising the Mishnah and Gemera[6]) says, "As the fishes in the sea immediately perish when they come out of the water, so do men perish when they separate themselves from the words of Torah."[7]

When a young Jewish boy or girl would enter synagogue school for the very first time, the synagogue teacher would put honey on their tablet and instruct the child to eat the honey. Wilson describes this practice in *Our Father Abraham*: "…[the child's] slate was coated with honey, which he promptly licked off, being reminded of Ezekiel, who said after eating the scroll, 'I ate it and it tasted as sweet as honey to my mouth' (Ezek. 3:3)."[8] This emphasized greatly to the child that the Word of God was a delight and a joy, not a burden or something to study simply to appease God.

Let's be honest: When teenagers walk through our doors for the first time no one is thinking about handing them a honey packet and a tablet to draw their hearts toward loving the Word of God. We're often not primarily focused on the Word of God at all. Our priority tends to be creating a hyped-up atmosphere for teenagers. Handing them a few free things, grabbing their attention through a high-charged, fun atmosphere. Hoping it keeps them involved for the long haul.

But do "hype" and "devotion" have to be enemies?

The "Fun" Factory

I don't think there's anything wrong with free stuff. I love free stuff. But we need to think about what we're communicating to teenagers through our behavior and words. These are two very different messages: *taste and see that the Lord is good* vs. *come here to get cool, free stuff and have a hyped-up, awesome time.* Teenagers can have a hyped-up, awesome time at a friend's house or sporting event. They

(Both?)

need—and want—something deeper, and as youth workers it's one of our responsibilities to offer that to them.

Someone much smarter than me (the apostle Paul) once wrote, "a man reaps what he sows" (Galatians 6:7). If I expect to be a disciple maker but am constantly sending the message that I am a fun factory, I will reap what I sow and continue to be frustrated as to why I'm not making disciples. However, if you do throw a curveball at your ministry practices by teaching deeper truths and focusing more on Scripture, don't be surprised when a few people miss the fun factory and hop on the "complain train."

I remember talking to a parent whose child said she didn't want to come now because "it wasn't fun anymore." I respectfully asked her, "When your child wakes up in the morning, do you give her the option of not going to school?" "Well of course not," this parent said. "She needs to be in school." "Even if it's not 'fun' anymore?" I asked. She got where I was coming from, and I saw her daughter in youth group the very next week.

Now, I'm not suggesting we should remove all fun from youth ministry. In fact, I think youth ministry should be fun! I'm simply saying that if we want to make disciples, fun cannot be our primary focus. As Richard Ross writes in his book *Student Ministry and the Supremacy of Christ*,

> A new standard for viable youth ministry should be not the number of attenders, the sophistication of events, or the "cool" factor of the youth group but whether teens have the commitment, passion and resources to pursue Christ intentionally and whole-heartedly after they leave the youth ministry nest.[9]

This will take a lot more time and investment on our part. However, the results will bring about lasting fruit.

We all know that the best relationships grow through ongoing conversations. If my husband and I aren't communicating well, our relationship suffers. If we're communicating with regularity and as friends, then our marriage grows and flourishes. God has given us ways of communicating with him as well, and one of them is through studying, understanding, and wrestling with his Word.

What's Your Focus?

I'm involved in a few youth pastor groups on social media, and I just looked through one of those pages. The main topics of conversation tend to settle around questions such as "What's your youth space like?" and "How do I get kids to come back to youth group?" and "What's a fun lock-in activity?" There was only one post among many that asked about a good curriculum for studying the Bible with teens, and I had to sift through nearly thirty posts before I found it.

We tend to believe the lie that says we need to attract teens to our youth groups—but the Spirit of God is what draws people. Our actual responsibility is to share the message, to pray, and to live a life that is devoted to God. This is what attracts others to want to know who God is. Maybe some of our problem is that we ourselves find studying the Word of God boring. Yet we must remember that what was true for the biblical heroes of old is true for us today. As Garr writes, beautiful things happen when we spend time in the Word: "As they studied what God had already communicated to His servants, they received additional insights into His will and purposes for their own time and were thereby empowered to accomplish God's designs for their lives and communities."[10] Studying God's Word is empowering—and it doesn't have to be boring.

Until we show through our own lives that knowing, studying, and understanding the Word of God is a life-changing experience, we will make very few disciples. What are you calling your teenagers to be part of? Is it something that will transform their lives, or just something that's fun for a little while? And if it's something fun, is that fun simply one more thing to do, smashed into an already over-busy life? How can we give our teenagers something that lasts and truly matters?

An Active Faith

The Hebrew word Shema, which we looked at earlier in terms of memorizing and knowing Scripture, is often translated in English as "hear," but it would be better translated as "listen." In *Walking in the Dust of Rabbi Jesus*, Lois Tverberg writes, "the word Shema actually has a much wider, deeper meaning than 'to perceive sound.' It encompasses a whole spectrum of ideas that includes listening, taking heed, and responding with action to what one has heard."[11] Hearing from God was an activity, not something that was passive. Faith, at its best, should be radically active, as it was for the Jewish people of the first century.

True devotion was shown to me by a teenager during his bar mitzvah in Jerusalem back in 2011. Little did he know his actions spoke loud and clear, telling me that he was radically and passionately devoted to the study of God's Word. Are we just as radically devoted to Jesus and his Word? Or is his Word another passive formality in the midst of our busy ministry schedules, something we don't look at much at all or only spend time with out of a sense of duty or obligation?

I know you've probably felt it, the struggle to pick a topic to teach on based on the current struggles your teens are facing. However, no message you can give on why it's bad to drink, smoke, or have premarital sex will do much good if they do not have a love for Jesus and his Word.

When you think about what you're teaching your teenagers, consider the following:

1. Make a switch away from topical teaching toward teaching through a book of the Bible.
2. Don't get distracted by the latest, greatest teaching on whatever.
3. Don't struggle over finding the perfect piece of multimedia to accompany your message, spending major amounts of time trying to find a cool teaching video or movie clip. Focus the majority of your time and energy on becoming a student of God's

Word.

4. Model a life of devotion to Jesus by the way you study and apply his Word. If we're excited about God's Word, others will follow suit.

5. Bring teens into an experience with God as you teach. Be creative, using different teaching methods and practices. Consider taking them outside of the classroom or youth room (more on this later).

Go ahead, take it to the next level with your teens. Trust me, they'll respond. I've seen it happen.

Experiencing the Story

The word Shema denotes active participation. In a similar way, devout Jewish people of the first century believed that God was meant not just to be known, but to be experienced. This is why the majority of the time when we read about Jesus and his disciples they're going somewhere or doing something—together. Wilson writes, "Jesus discipled his followers in the fashion of a typical first-century itinerant teacher of Judaism. Not in the synagogue classrooms but on hillsides, in fields, and in remote locations."[12] We never read, "Jesus and his disciples were sitting in the classroom again," or "Look, there's Jesus and his disciples studying for the Torah test together, making sure their brains can store all the information necessary to pass the test." Yes, the first few years for nearly every practicing Jew were spent in the classroom, but there came a point in time when they began going outside of the classroom and started to experience God's Torah in real life. For a first-century Jew, following God wasn't about passing the test. It was about entering into an ongoing, life-changing experience with the living God.

I'm an experiential learner. I love listening to stories, and telling them. One of my least favorite things is to sit in a classroom and have someone share endless amounts of information with me through an old PowerPoint in Times New Roman font. This is why my time in Israel was so life-changing: I was able to see and experience something that no PowerPoint presentation could ever convey. At every twist and turn I was experiencing the Word of God coming to life.

Think about taking your teens on a journey through God's Word. Bring them out of the classroom and into an experience. Go serve a widow in your church and put the words of Scripture into practice while doing so: "Religion that God our Father accepts as pure and faultless is this: to look after orphans and widows in their distress and to keep oneself from being polluted by the world" (James 1:27).

Instead of sitting in a circle talking about caring for the vulnerable, go and do it! Read the Word of God and then put feet to it, letting it come alive for you and your teenagers. Really think about what you're communicating to your teens by what you're providing them each week during your programming. What do your games, announcements, small groups, messages, songs, or giveaways communicate about God? Does any part of your ministry communicate the importance and goodness of a life devoted to God and his Word? Is anyone modeling that kind of life to your teens? Are you?

Let teenagers taste and see that the Lord is good. As you, their youth leader, help provide the tools and resources for them to grow in their relationship with God, you'll notice some of them develop a true passion for him.

First-Century Youth Ministry

The Disciples' Passion

Growing up, I was extremely passionate about sports. At nearly every chance I got I was outside either shooting a basketball, throwing a softball, or running around something to win a prize. Quite frankly, sports consumed most of my life as a child. Sports were something my dad was very passionate about too. Wanting to be like him, I followed in his footsteps. I knew in order to excel at athletics I had to have a relentless devotion to my sport, so I would spend hours out in the driveway shooting hoops. I also spent a crazy amount of time on the golf course trying to improve my game. I knew the names of the women on the Olympic softball team and wanted to be just like them, so my glove and bat had those women's names on them. I once went to a game where Dot Richardson, a former Team USA softball athlete, was playing. My sister and I waited after the game for her to sign our ball. When she passed back that bright yellow softball with her signature on it, it felt like someone was handing me a piece of gold. I treasured that ball for many years.

We're going to take a look at a different sort of passion: a disciple's devotion and commitment to become just like their rabbi. While I was in Israel, John referred to this as "the disciples' passion." My prayer and hope are that you will be overwhelmed with a desire to become just like your Rabbi Jesus, propelled forward to pursue him with complete and total devotion.

During my time in ministry, I had the joy of ministering to a teenager named Kendell who shared the disciples' passion. Kendell was at the church every time the doors were open. There was a hunger inside of him that inspired me to follow Jesus with that same kind of radical obedience. I'm fairly certain that if Jesus were to show up on the scene today and go looking for disciples, he'd choose Kendell to be one of them.

Kendell was someone I and other leaders saw mature in faith before our very eyes. I watched him take courageous steps as he started overcoming deep fears in his life. Not only that, but Kendell was passionate about sharing his faith with others. He lost some friends over his devotion to Jesus, as they chose to walk a different path, but that didn't keep Kendell from pursuing the Lord. As he grew spiritually, he started co-leading the morning prayer group at the high school and opened up to our youth ministry by sharing his own struggles with loneliness and depression. Kendell shared with our group about his struggles with sin, what that looked like in his life, and how he wanted to live differently. Kendell did what any true disciple would have done: He took profound steps of faith, because his life was fully devoted to Jesus.

As Jesus traveled around the Judean countryside, he went looking for disciples, which in Hebrew are called *talmidim* (plural) or *talmid* (singular). The Jewish people understood that following a rabbi required a commitment that involved a person's whole being. Being a disciple meant accepting a challenge to give up everything to be just like the rabbi. Ray Vander Laan, a well-known teacher and scholar of first-century Judaism, writes the following about the day-in and day-out commitment a *talmid* would make to their rabbi:

> A *talmid* followed the rabbi everywhere, often without knowing or asking where he was going. He rarely left his rabbi's side for fear that he would miss a teachable moment. And he watched the rabbi's every move, noting how he acted and thought about a variety of situations.[1]

Furthermore, he adds, "the disciples' deepest desire was to follow their rabbi so closely that they would start to think and act like him."[2]

In our culture, we use a different approach in our schools and youth groups. When we want to share information, we'll put together an awesome teaching lesson or get kids to check off boxes on a test at school, thinking that we have made them good disciples or good learners. Sadly, sometimes our best efforts actually end up snuffing out the disciples' passion in young people.

In the culture Jesus lived in, being a disciple meant something much deeper than simply calling yourself one. Marv Wilson writes that "in Hebrew thought to 'know' something was to experience it."[3] In other words, knowledge and experience went hand in hand. This is not common in our culture. Someone who shares the energy and commitment we call the disciples' passion is a person who's looking to experience the power of God. Some of our youth ministry programs lack the true power of God because bringing teenagers into an experience with the living God isn't our focus.

This is something I began thinking about a lot while I was in Israel. I didn't know how to move forward. I asked John for advice. "What should I do?" I wondered. "How can I bring what I've experienced into my youth ministry setting?"

"Heather," he said, "the first thing I would do is take your students on a walk, but don't tell them where you're going. After a while in silence and after you've gone some distance say to them, 'This is what it's like to follow Jesus. It means trusting him no matter where you're going. It means following him even though you don't know the destination.'" John was challenging me to take teenagers out of the classroom and into an experience. He was exhorting me to bring faith into action, teaching my teens what following a rabbi must have really been like.

The Greatest Commandment

The greatest commandment in Scripture helps us better understand what it meant in the past, and can mean now, to share in the disciples' passion. When asked, Jesus says the greatest commandment is this: "Love the Lord your God with all your heart and with all your soul and with all your mind and with all your strength" (Mark 12:30).

The original Hebrew word for soul is *nephesh*. *Nephesh* refers to something that encompasses every part of you, hitting at the deepest part of your inner being. In Sunday school, I taught our teenagers about the word *nephesh*. I had them imagine being Clark Kent becoming Superman, ripping open his button-down shirt to reveal his true identity. We each also have an inner self that we are growing for God, I explained. This inner being can grow as we learn to love the Lord with every single part of ourselves. With all of our *nephesh*. We can become Supermen and Superwomen for God! In doing so, we teach others how to grow the same kind of inner-person, living with the disciples' passion.

Looking for Talmid

The first-century Jewish community put learning into action. When a devout Jew learned, they were expected to apply their knowledge. To learn without application was not considered learning at all. "A *talmid* didn't just repeat what the teacher said, they emulated in every way what the teacher is," I remember John telling us one day in Israel. As Garr writes, "Originally the word *talmid* was applied to a student of music. This, of course, confirms to us that the disciple was not merely a repository for knowledge, for music is enjoyed only when it is performed."[4]

In the first century, to be a *talmid* meant that your life was set apart. It meant something radical. It required not only someone's intellect, but their time, energy, and devotion. It required the disciples' passion, like what I saw in Kendell. Just as a devout Jewish person would have been devoted to the study of the Torah, the following of a rabbi would have required the same type of commitment and passion.

The Call to Follow

I believe North American youth ministry has missed the mark on making disciples because we spend our best efforts coming up with the most cutting-edge programs. When teenagers are attending those programs that's often enough to make us feel accomplished—but is anyone's heart swelling with the disciples' passion? I have found that when my heart is focused on growing the ministry through high-energy programs, my own passion for Jesus starts to die at the hands of my self-inflicted exhaustion. Imagine if Jesus had spent all his time investing into a weekly program, going all in on a couple of hours packed with high-octane fun and a slam-dunk lesson—and then called it good until the next week. I'm sure he would have gathered some large crowds and put together some pretty awesome events, but would he have made disciples who changed the world?

As a rabbi, Jesus was someone who embodied the Torah. He was, in every way, a living example of God's Word. He embodied what it meant to live with the disciples' passion. Rabbis in his time were fiercely devoted to God through their study and understanding of Scripture—and that's what drew people to them. Their love and devotion to God is what made people want to be their disciples. Tverberg and Spangler write,

> A disciple apprenticed himself to a rabbi because the rabbi had saturated his life with Scripture and had become a true follower of God. The disciple sought to study the text, not only of Scripture but of the rabbi's life, for it was there that he would learn how to live out the Torah. Even more than acquiring his master's knowledge, he wanted to acquire his master's character, his internal grasp of God's law.[5]

What about you? How are you attracting teens into your ministry? Is it through fun, games, loudspeakers, and awesome food? Or is it through a life so devoted to Jesus that others are desperate to know him like you do? It's no wonder people left everything to follow Jesus. He was the most exciting person on the planet, and it wasn't because he had Lecrae on speed dial or a lifelong deal with Domino's for free pizza.

The disciples—the *talmidim*—sacrificed their lives to be just like their rabbi. In the first century, to give anything less than your whole self to your rabbi would have been considered disgraceful. That's why it's so painful when Peter denies Jesus three times. In Israel we learned that denying your rabbi three times in public was the same as saying "I am completely done with this person; they are dead to me." What about us as youth pastors and youth leaders? Are we sacrificing our lives to be just like our Rabbi Jesus? Or could it be that we're sacrificing our walk with God to find fulfillment in outwardly successful ministries instead?

Teenagers Like Kendell

How do we get more teenagers like Kendell in our ministries? For one thing, we have to be strategic in everything we do. If we truly want to make *talmidim*, then we must be willing to set the bar high, with lots and lots of grace for when our teenagers make mistakes. This is how Jesus did it. Even after Peter's denial, Jesus extended grace to him, reinstated him, and gave him even more leadership responsibilities. Our teens are going to fail too, so lots of grace will be needed. We must challenge them to take up brand-new lives of radical devotion to the Lord Jesus.

I can recall a teenager I had in my ministry. You could tell that he was toeing the line, not sure if he wanted to dive all the way in as a leader for Christ, but I knew he had the leadership qualities that if he did, God would use him greatly. I remember talking with him one day after he had been struggling in his faith and had made some pretty poor decisions. I said to him, "I want you to know that I believe in you. It's okay to fail, because I fail a lot too. We are here for you in the youth ministry, we love you, care about you and believe in you. I know that God is going to use your life greatly." I wanted to make sure he understood that I believed he had what it took to be used by God. Later that year I even challenged him to go into ministry, because I sensed the Lord impressing upon me to share that with him. I took the opportunity to challenge him by calling him up and calling him into a more radical life with Jesus. Now, this young man didn't respond as I hoped he would during that season, but I'm praying and hoping that someday, he will.

The Great Commission

The Great Commission is what many people claim as their ethos for discipleship. I wonder, however, if we truly understand, from a first-century context, just what Jesus meant when he left us with that final command: "Therefore go and make disciples of all nations, baptizing them in the name of the Father and of the Son and of the Holy Spirit" (Matthew 28:19). Many of us look to this Scripture to formulate our purpose for discipleship. We say things like, "We want to make disciples who make disciples." That is good, but do we understand, fully, what Jesus is asking of us when he says to go and "make disciples"?

If we think of what the word disciple—or *talmid*, as we looked at earlier—would have meant to people in the first century, we can better understand the Great Commission. At its root, the word *talmid* means pupil or learner. At that time, the word carried an implication of devotion and discipline. To call oneself a *talmid* was to place oneself in a position of humility, as a student before your teacher. Do we see this in our own teenagers? If we truly want to make disciples who make disciples, we must first create an atmosphere that reproduces teachers *and* learners. Truly, we've missed the mark on what it means to make a disciple if we have not made learning part of our ministry praxis.

As a basketball referee with only a few short years under my belt I knew that in order to grow as an official I had to first become a learner. I had to observe people with more experience than me so I could grow in my trade. Once I did, not only did I improve as an official, but I became part of something bigger than myself—a network of other officials who were there to support and encourage me. I grew into a better official thanks to their investment in me. Growing as a disciple has a lot more to do with learning than we may think.

Becoming a disciple is no small calling, either. As I previously mentioned, the word for disciple carried an implication of devotion and discipline. Jesus asks a rich man to sell all he has and then come follow him. He challenges his listeners to take up their cross daily and follow him, because without doing so, they cannot be his disciples. 1 John 2:6 says, "whoever claims to live in him must live as Jesus did." The rich man was unwilling to sell his possessions. The call to be a true disciple is easy in words, but hard in practice. In the long run, having a fuller understanding of the word disciple not only challenges us as youth workers to raise the bar of commitment and devotion and learning for ourselves, but also gives teenagers an opportunity to see someone who's living as one of the disciples described within the Great Commission.

The Age of the Disciples

This invitation from Jesus to become *talmidim* was extended to a group of young people who changed the world. There have been questions and debates about the age of the disciples. A typical depiction in our Western world shows them to be old and bald, hunched over with a slight case of scoliosis. Based on these pictures the average person would understandably assume that the disciples were middle-aged men, probably in their forties or fifties. However, a deeper look at the Scriptures and the practices in the first century reveals a very different reality.

Most Jewish girls would start out in primary school and finish up by the age of ten. Jewish boys would continue on, but only the best of the best would get to the point where they followed a rabbi. If they weren't the best of the best, then they would no longer continue on in the Jewish educational system and would instead start working in their father's trade. Tverberg and Spangler observe,

> By the age of thirteen most boys would have concluded their formal study and then begun to learn a trade. The most talented among them would have been encouraged to continue studying throughout their teenage years at the *bet midrash* ("house of interpretation") at the synagogue until they married at the age of eighteen or twenty. Only the most brilliant would go on to become disciples of a great rabbi.[6]

The most elite students would approach a rabbi and ask if they could follow him. By observing a rabbi's life, the potential disciples would have an idea of who they wanted to follow. It's important to note that the rabbis were observing the students too. If a student came to a rabbi and requested to follow him, and the rabbi didn't believe the student had what it took to do so, the rabbi had every right to say no. Here's the cool thing about Jesus, though: He flips it all around. Instead of waiting for people to come to him, Jesus approaches people and asks them to follow him. In essence, Jesus says, "I think that you can be like me." And if you notice, Jesus doesn't go to the synagogue looking for the most elite students. He goes to the students no longer in the Jewish educational system. He goes to the dropouts, the ones who hadn't made the cut! He goes to the people who are working in their fathers' trades and calls them to be his followers! It's no wonder they drop everything to follow after Jesus.

The disciples were not old men. They weren't even middle-aged. Some may have been teenagers. (I believe this to be the case. In Matthew 17 only Peter and Jesus pay the temple tax that was required for people twenty years old and older. This indicates that the other disciples were all nineteen or younger.) Not only that, but the typical age for someone to begin following a rabbi was around eighteen. Since Jesus followed the customs and culture of his day, we can safely assume that these young men (except for Peter) were in fact teenagers. Jesus called young people to come and be like him. He called them to change the world, and he's calling young people today to go and do the same.

A Brand-New Calling

I think it's time to rethink the words we use and the invitations we give our teenagers. In the typical vernacular, we might invite our teens to "ask Jesus into your heart and be saved." What if instead we said something like this? "Jesus thinks that you can be like him. He's calling you to a brand-new life. It's a radical life where you let go of everything to become just like him."

Jesus isn't looking for the brightest and the best intellectuals. He looks into the heart. We can see this in the story of God calling David to be

47

the next king of Israel in 1 Samuel 16. The prophet Samuel is told by God to go to Jesse's house and anoint a new king. Samuel sees many strong, capable sons of Jesse, but finds no man worthy of kingship. Being strong and capable are not the traits God sought. Israel's future king, Jesse's youngest son, was out in the shepherd's field. It was not his stature, accomplishments, or prestige that made David God's chosen king. God saw in David the heart of a shepherd, tending to, protecting, feeding, and caring for his flock. In light of a story like this, it's no surprise that Jesus bypasses the most exceptional students in the synagogue and goes looking for disciples on a fishing boat and in a tax collector's booth.

 Maybe some of your teenagers feel like their upbringing, family, or failures make them unworthy of being Jesus's disciples. Remind them that it's not their strength, stature, or prestige that make them worthy. It's God's grace through the Holy Spirit that empowers them to become like Jesus.

There's another teenager I know who shares the disciples' passion. Her name is Brynn. I think she would have been one of the women who found herself in the company of Jesus. She's a *talmidah* (female disciple) and is another one of those teenagers who is at the church every time the doors are open. She really loves Jesus and wants to be like him in every way possible. The thing I appreciate the most about Brynn is that she's quick to admit her failures. For a while, she strayed from Jesus and made some bad choices along the way. The cool thing about Brynn is that in her repentance, she's sharing her story with others with the hopes that they won't make some of the same decisions she did. That's the kind of heart that God is looking for, a heart of humility. After all, in the company of Jesus were a doubter, a traitor, a big mouth, a couple of really prideful brothers, and a former prostitute. These are the kinds of people to whom Jesus said, "Come, follow me."

If Jesus showed up on the scene today, he wouldn't go to the prestigious, aged pastors who've written a number of books, spoken on many podcasts, and built large ministries for themselves. He'd go to your youth group and look for a Kendell or a Brynn. He'd look for teenagers with hearts like David's, Joshua's, Ruth's, and Esther's. He'd go searching for the ones who might be overlooked in other areas of their lives, but who want to be just like Jesus in every way possible.

First-Century Youth Ministry

The Keys to the Kingdom

Not long ago, I walked through a season of transition where I stepped away from a long-term ministry I was leading to enter into a period of rest and healing. For the ten years before this point, I had been someone who held the actual physical keys to the church; after all, I was working on staff. The day I turned those keys in was painful because now I no longer had full access to the church whenever I wanted. By simply giving back the keys I once held, my influence shrank within that church body.

Through this season of transition my husband and I started serving at a different church. If I needed to get into the building, I'd have to go during office hours or make sure someone could let me in. After a few months attending that church I started leading a girls Bible study, and I went from "keyless" to "key holder" almost overnight. Something about receiving that new set of keys made me feel like I was more of an insider, and that I had more significance within the church. It's not that I was looking for power, but let's be honest: When you have the keys, you can do more.

I understood that receiving those keys came with great responsibility, and I'm immensely thankful that the church entrusted me with them. They believed in what I was doing and giving me those keys was a real but also symbolic show of their support.

Unlocking Keychain Leadership

In the book *Growing Young,* one of the six essential growth strategies for churches that are attracting and keeping young people is identified as "unlocking keychain leadership." This means, in other words, "instead of centralizing authority, empower others—especially young people."[1] The keys are "the capabilities, power, and access of the leaders that carry the potential to empower young people" and leaders who know how to empower young people with the keys of the church are "intentional about entrusting and empowering all generations, including teenagers and emerging adults, with their own set of keys."[2]

With all of this in mind, we can see that it's no small thing that Jesus handed the keys of leadership—the call to take the gospel to the ends of the earth—to a group of young people who ended up transforming the world through his power.

When Jesus came to the region of Caesarea Philippi, he asked his disciples, "Who do people say the Son of Man is?"

They replied, "Some say John the Baptist; others say Elijah; and still others, Jeremiah or one of the prophets."

"But what about you?" he asked. "Who do you say I am?"

Simon Peter answered, "You are the Messiah, the Son of the living God."

Jesus replied, "Blessed are you, Simon son of Jonah, for this was not revealed to you by flesh and blood, but by my Father in heaven. And I tell you that you are Peter, and on this rock, I will build my church, and the gates of Hades will not overcome it. I will give you the keys of the kingdom of heaven; whatever you bind on earth will be bound in heaven, and whatever you loose on earth will be loosed in heaven." Then he ordered his disciples

not to tell anyone that he was the Messiah.
(Matthew 16:13-20)

We see in this passage that Jesus was going to heaven, and he was passing on the mantle of leadership to his disciples. Yes, that's right: He passed the baton to young people, mainly teenagers. He entrusted them with one of the greatest responsibilities in the world: to use those keys to unlock the gospel message to all people groups—to the ends of the earth. You and I hold similar keys, keys of authority that can help propel a young person into leadership. The gift of these keys offers the opportunity to trust God more fully.

Can you imagine how scared the disciples must have been in that moment at Caesarea Philippi when Jesus said to them, "I will give you the keys of the kingdom of heaven" (Matthew 16:19)? I wonder if they even fully understood the magnitude of what Jesus was saying.

Empower Young People to Lead

In the Jewish world, Caesarea Philippi was a pagan place. It was where the Greeks worshipped a fertility God named Pan. The Jewish people believed the gates of Hades were located there.[3] So, when they're in this place and Jesus says that the gates of Hades shall not prevail against his church, and then passes the disciples the keys of authority, from a first-century Jewish perspective Jesus was saying, "You're going to bring the gospel to places like this, and through my power it will prevail!"

Your teens are facing their own Caesarea Philippi. Give them the keys and the strategies to reach those places for the Lord Jesus. Empower them, just as Jesus did for his disciples, to bring the hope of the gospel to the most sinful places in all the world. Sometimes, that journey starts with the locker room, the cheerleading team, or an after-school job. Any of those could be the Caesarea Philippi God is calling them to.

The journey of faith that our teenagers are traveling is hard and even confusing. That's why it's so important that we serve as guides to them, training them up and preparing them for the keys of leadership. Not all of our teenagers will be ready to embrace such a role, and some won't want anything to do with it. However, there will be a few ready to take up the call.

Growing Young asserts that "keychain leaders, very aware of the keys they hold, are constantly opening doors for some while training and entrusting others who are ready for their own set of keys."[4] Being someone who shares the keys requires humility and trust. If you're a key-hoarding leader, it probably means you have some control and fear issues. I have been that key-hoarding, controlling leader. Sometimes I was afraid to share the keys because I felt like others would start liking other key-holders more than me, and that would make me replaceable. The writers of *Growing Young* found that for people who moved from key-hoarding to key-sharing, "their maturity was born out of difficult personal and professional experience, failure, and other struggles."[5] Yep, that's been me too. God usually has to bring very humbling circumstances into our lives for us to wake up and see our own pride. He's done it in my life. I'm learning that the best kind of Christlike leader is one who shares the keys and makes the ministry not about serving their own ego, but about serving others and highlighting their gifts.

One of the very best youth leaders I've ever worked with is a guy named Mike, whose wisdom on this I learned a lot from. Mike would always say to me, "Heather, you've got to share this youth ministry with so many people and give so many others the opportunity to lead that people don't know who the leader is." I believe this is something all of us should strive for. Once I started applying this principle to my ministry setting, not only did more people want to be on my team, but they felt more valued and like they had greater ownership of the ministry.

Do Your Part

As we looked at in chapter three, Jesus stood before his disciples one last time before ascending into heaven and gave them one command: to go and make disciples. In other words, he commissioned them to go and make more *talmidim*, teaching, training, and equipping others for kingdom work. One of the saddest realities in the modern church is that we are often so caught up in programs that we forget how Jesus went about his ministry. We forget that Jesus's message started in a small fishing town, and that it was his faithfully investing in a few, entrusting them with the keys of leadership, that led them to go out and do their part to change the world. Jesus's disciples certainly didn't reach everyone in their lifetimes, but because of their faithfulness to *do their part* in the kingdom of God, the gospel continues to spread unto the ends of the earth.

We need to find ways of passing on the keys of leadership to young people. But what does this really require? It means that we have to let go of the idea that church needs to be about running some impressive-looking program. It should instead be a training ground for young people to try, fail, and try again. In his book *Teenagers Matter*, Mark Cannister writes, "Nothing is more reflective of healthy student ministries than students who launch into the full and robust life of the church."[6] In order for this to happen, though, the broader church must be prepared for and committed to receiving teenagers into its midst by valuing them for who they are and allowing them to contribute to the whole life of the church.

I don't think any of us intends to convey to our teens that we don't want them to be leaders in the church. In fact, I think the youth ministry community is trying with all its might to engage young people in leadership. Yet, when we give compelling messages to our teenagers encouraging them to step up and be leaders for Christ, are we then actually shepherding them into leadership roles? Or are we just giving them a youth Sunday tacked onto an insignificant week of the year?

I'm Bringing Bar Mitzvah/Bat Mitzvah Back

Here's one of the things I love about Jewish culture: There are lots of watershed moments young people walk through in their spiritual development, leading them on a journey toward maturity. Take, for example, the bar mitzvah ceremony (for a boy) or bat mitzvah ceremony (for a girl). In their book *Traditions,* Dr. Avram Davis and Sara Shendelman write,

> The Bar or Bat Mitzvah is the Jewish rite of passage from childhood to adulthood that occurs at the age of thirteen…This time is also one of initiation into the Jewish community as a responsible man or woman of duty, or a son or daughter of the commandments.[7]

During a bar mitzvah or bat mitzvah ceremony these twelve- to thirteen-year-old Jewish boys and girls are surrounded by peers, mentors, and family members who make the commitment to walk alongside them in their faith journey. After these rites of passage, the Jewish community treats these thirteen-year-olds as adults, no longer as children. Thus, the message comes through loud and clear to these young people that their faith has to become their own. They are expected to mature as full members in the synagogue and in the community of faith.

Think about your youth ministry. Are you communicating a similar message to your teens? Are there any rites of passage or coming-of-age ceremonies for young people in your ministry, leading them toward maturity?

A number of years ago, a dad in my youth ministry planned a rite of passage for his thirteen-year-old son. He gathered a number of older men in the congregation for what he called a "Becoming a Man Ceremony." He held this special event on a piece of farmland owned by one of the men in our church. Throughout the night this young man walked along the land, encountering on his way different men who shared Godly, biblical wisdom with him. At the end of the ceremony, all of the men gathered and prayed over this young man, initiating him into biblical manhood, giving him the charge to grow into maturity as a man of God.

Depending on your church tradition, your congregation likely makes vows when a baby is dedicated or baptized, or during a confirmation ceremony. But what do we do beyond that to walk alongside our young people in fostering their faith development? What processes are we creating for our teens that give them opportunities to receive the keys of leadership?

When Are They Ready for the Keys?

Let's take a closer look at the disciples Jesus led. What made them ready to be entrusted with their own set of keys, and how does that apply to the teens in our ministries?

1. **They were growing in maturity.** In the Jewish world Jesus lived in, a boy was considered a man at the age of thirteen and he was treated as such. A girl was considered a woman at the time of her first menstrual cycle, also around the age of thirteen, and she would marry soon after that. Because their society already treated them as adults, to us today the disciples would seem mature for their age.

   When you think about the teenagers you'd be willing to pass keys to, look for the ones who are growing in maturity. Maybe it's not yet the right time to pass the church keys off to that junior high kid who holds the record for the longest burp. Look for a young person who is taking ownership of his or her faith and putting it into practice.

2. **They had been trained up.** Before I even got my learner's permit, I practiced out on backroads with my dad. He would let me steer and press the gas pedal from the passenger seat. The backroads were where my dad gave me my first training tips. More formal instruction and practice followed after that. I spent many hours in driver's ed, being trained up by people who knew how to drive. The day I got my license I was ready for the set of keys to the car. It is our responsibility to help train up the future generations of the church, preparing them for the opportunities and responsibilities to come.

3. **They were devoted to their rabbi.** The teenagers who are ready for a set of keys are fiercely devoted to Jesus. Be looking for those young people and start investing in them right away. There's a teen in my former ministry named Tyler. When I first met Tyler,

he was shy, a little socially awkward, but very talkative one-on-one. He was extremely afraid of speaking in larger gatherings, but one day with some help from a friend he got up in front of our group and started sharing. It built up from there. He just kept doing this, sharing more and more, until sometimes it felt like Tyler was giving short sermon to his peers. He showed a radical commitment to Jesus and he was blossoming as a leader for Christ right in front of us. Tyler was ready for keys.

4. **They had spent most of their lives as students, studying the Word of God.** Having grown up in the Jewish educational system, most of the disciples would have spent the majority of their time as young children learning the words of the Torah. Our teens may not have been memorizing large passages of Scripture since early childhood, but the best teachers and leaders are people who are committed to being students. After all, being a pupil or learner is at the heart of the definition of the word *talmid*.

But how do you know who to pick? You can't invest your life in forty students in this way. Jesus had only twelve disciples and of those twelve, three were closest to him. I recently had a conversation with my senior pastor that touched on this. "Heather," he said, "I have concluded that I am completely fine with having favorites. Those are the people I invest in the most." I'll be honest—I've had my favorites too. There's nothing wrong with having some teenagers, or maybe even adult leaders, who you connect with more. You don't have to be everything for everyone. You will likely connect especially with certain young people, and other teens may connect more easily with other adult leaders. That is how it's supposed to work.

When you think about who you're going to invest in, take your time, be strategic, and understand that it's going to be messy. Discipleship is always messy. I mean, look at Jesus's group. One of them completely betrays him and hands him over to be arrested, another denies him three times, and still another is considered a doubter. That sounds like messy discipleship to me, but that's what happens when we get deeply involved in the lives of others. We bring our mess, they bring theirs, and we do our best to have grace for one another as we do life together. I've had moments as a leader where I've had to ask for forgiveness from my volunteers and teenagers. After all, we're real people too, not divinely anointed spiritual leaders set above the rest. Each of us would be one of Jesus's messy disciples. In fact, he'd probably nickname me "the messy one." Thankfully, he loves all the messy ones like you and me.

Choose Wisely: Take Your Time

This is the crazy thing I've learned about Jesus after following him for over fifteen years: He really does listen to our prayers. I know this sounds elementary, but sometimes my life doesn't reflect my belief in how he listens. I've been quick to jump ahead, start programs, and take needless action to deal with the belief that I am failing to meet others' expectations of me and "I need to do something about it." Instead of listening to God and waiting on him, I've jumped the gun and run a million miles ahead of him, only to end up worn out and exhausted.

Take your time. Pray. Look for the young people whose hearts are passionate for God. Pay close attention to the teens you have a deeper connection with. Remember, it's okay to have favorites. Start asking God to show you which people he wants you to invest your life in further. Ask, wait, pray, and maybe wait some more. Once you've done all of that, start investing in the lives of the ones you feel God calling you to, and as they mature, look for ways to pass off a set of keys.

Here are practical ways to pass off keys to some of your teenagers:

1. Ask a teen to be in charge of audiovisual needs each week. I had a teenager, Trenton, who edited all of my teaching videos and prepared them for me. He also ran the soundboard for the church service on Sunday mornings. As he was trusted with more, Trenton started growing in his faith, and his leadership skills started to flourish right before us. He even got up and preached on one youth Sunday. We gave him a few keys at first and he just kept proving himself, so when youth Sunday rolled around, he

was ready (with a little coaching) to deliver a great message.

2. Hold a youth Sunday. On these Sunday mornings I've had teenagers do dramas, assist in worship, preach, lead prayers, and serve communion. They took on important roles in the church service. Remember that it will take time to help them get ready for this kind of responsibility, and resist the urge to be a key-hoarder, filling the most significant spots yourself. Investing in teens by being a key-sharer takes more time, but it is worth it.

3. Help teens start and lead a prayer group at their school. They might need some help, but once they get things going, entrust them with it and guide them along the way. Remember Kendell and Brynn from my ministry? They started a before-school group at their high school. Each Monday morning they'd gather together, read a devotional, and circle up for prayer. They led all of this themselves. I just brought the doughnuts.

4. Get your senior leadership on board. Have a conversation with your senior pastor or other leaders to look for ways to get teenagers plugged into serving within the church on a regular basis. This might mean running the soundboard, taking video, updating social media, leading prayer time, helping with announcements, ushering, handing out bulletins, or greeting people as they walk in the doors of the church.

5. Start a student leadership group. During my last year at my previous church I gave my teens an opportunity to put leadership into action this way. They came up with the ideas and I provided the resources to make them happen. Through what they came up with, we held fundraisers, shared the gospel at the local high school, passed out free hot chocolate, and sent thank you cards to all the local teachers. These were all their own ideas and they were the ones making them happen.

6. Encourage your parents and youth leaders to hold "rite of passage" ceremonies, passing young people on from childhood to adulthood.

Once you start passing off keys, you'll experience some of your most rewarding moments in ministry as you see the gifts of young people put on display for the glory of God. Just think: You got to play a small part in helping them become who God created them to be. What a gift!

First-Century Youth Ministry

What is the role of parents in this?

Doing Life Together

Jesus modeled a ministry of "doing life together." When I write "doing life together" what I'm referring to is the practice of living discipleship out in community. It's the kind of life-on-life discipleship that Jesus and his disciples modeled, which was common in first-century Jewish culture. Community was so deeply embedded that it affected everything down to the individual letters of the Hebrew language, which live in community too: "No Hebrew letter ever stands alone," writes Abigail Wood. "If it's a single syllable it is either connected to what modifies it or it is given a friendly consonant to keep it company."[1] Wood continues, "This is a metaphor for Jewish community. No single member of the community stands alone."[2] Community and togetherness are deeply rooted in Jewish life.

Sadly, many students in this generation are standing alone. In his book *Hurt 2.0* Chap Clark concludes that "adolescents have been abandoned."[3] Clark pleads with adults to rally around teens and enter back into their worlds by investing once more in this generation of young people. Thankfully, there are some great youth ministries making a commitment to stand with teenagers and do just what Clark is challenging the youth ministry community to.

One of those places is New Life Fellowship in Moline, IL, where folks are taking the phrase "doing life together" to a whole new level. My friend Billy is the youth pastor at NLF and he has one of the most vibrant youth ministries in the area. The truth is, Billy and his wife, Katy, who is a volunteer with NLF, have taken their calling to love young people for the glory of God very seriously.

Each summer, I'm reminded of this when I see the awesome pictures Billy posts on his Facebook account. The pictures show Billy and Katy with a small group of teens on a summer trip they call Fusion. Every year Billy and Katy take a group on an intense, nearly monthlong discipleship experience, traveling throughout the United States, serving, praying, studying Scripture, and doing life together. When I look at their pictures my impression is that they're taking over the nation. One week they might be in Michigan; another week, they're in New York. The next week they're back home leading a huge outreach service and sharing the gospel with a room full of teenagers.

This past summer Billy asked me to come and share a teaching on discipleship with the Fusion group. After meeting with them and having a great time together, I asked Billy if he'd be willing to sit down and tell me more about this tremendous group of young people and what they were doing. Of course he said yes, and a couple weeks later, I walked into New Life Fellowship, weaving my way through the youth room and toward Billy's office where I was greeted by his two dogs, Wrigley and Chewy. Katy was sitting on the couch, ready to be part of the conversation.

I asked Billy about the group. "It started out of wanting to pour and invest into a group of students—to go deeper," he said. This more intensive experience of life together let everyone get to know each other in a fuller way. "They would see one aspect of me and my wife on a Wednesday night and I would see one aspect of them. It's easy for us to be one person then, but when they're with us 24/7 they get to see the real me. They get to see how married couples deal with conflict and how we blow it sometimes. How we have to apologize. We get to see how they are the other hours of the day."

Aside from Fusion, "We only see them for two hours, 52 weeks out of the year," Katy said. Having this extended time in the summer together made lots of new opportunities. "In this we get to go deep and have that quality time with one another," Katy said, adding that what keeps her hooked on participating in the Fusion experience is "seeing life change." Katy was thankful for a mentor who was involved in her life and said this group offers the opportunity for her to "pay it forward."

Billy and Katy's discipleship group is all about doing life together. There are three objectives they hope to accomplish through Fusion:

1. "A deeper experience with God. Where [the students] know God is real, so that when they blow it, they can go back to that time when God showed himself to them."

2. "Deeper, Christ-centered friendships that are built around the right things. Something happens when you're away together for three and a half to four weeks. I want students to have their best memories built around the things of God, with friends they'll have for the rest of their lives."

3. "What it's like to experience mission. We're experts at telling kids they have a purpose, but we suck at providing that for them. At Fusion we provide missions opportunities where they experience purpose through service projects. We might challenge them to pray for divine encounters through the month. After Fusion is over, they have a new sensitivity to be used by the Lord."

The authors of *Growing Young* write that "if we are going to empathize with today's young people, we have to explore these questions…. 'Who Am I? Where do I fit? What difference do I make?'"[4] Fusion helps teenagers answer questions like these. Billy and Katy's teenagers are growing in their understanding of God's purpose for their lives because of it.

During their weeks together, Billy, Katy, and their teens read the Bible, pray, and memorize Scripture together every day. Sometimes they even do wall sits while working on memorizing Scripture—the longer it takes for someone to quote a passage, the longer the team has to struggle. I imagine some of those kids had pretty ripped quads by the end of the summer! Billy says teenagers are not asked to attempt any of this alone. "As leaders, we're memorizing the Scripture too, so it's not like we're asking them to do something that we're not doing ourselves. It's incredible, the things that happen while we spend three and a half weeks together."

The teenagers who participate agree. I had the joy and privilege of sitting down with a few of them not too long ago on a wet and rainy Sunday evening at Billy and Katy's house. When I arrived the home was bustling with activity. There was a giant pile of shoes people had slipped off, the smell of Mexican food filled the air, and teenagers were everywhere. I loved every part of it and helped myself to some chips and salsa on my way through the kitchen.

What Teenagers Had to Say

Here's what these teens had to say about their Fusion trip:

- "It changes you from friends into family."
- "We were all just working together all of the time, like 24/7 for three and a half weeks. You just talk and learn about each other and make like a billion different inside jokes."
- "If you get mad at each other you have to work it out."
- "I would say it revolutionized my prayer life. When I started Fusion I was keeping up all my walls, and then I told everyone my story and I cried. I was prideful when it came to my relationship with God, because I was trying to hide that [what I went through] hurt that much. Being around so many supportive people really changes your outlook on life."
- "It was the first time I made real quality friends in the youth group, and I've been here for five years. It was the first time I felt close to the group."

"We felt really close together. There's something about it. It's more than just making friendships. You're just in God's presence together." Thanks to experiences like these, Billy and Katy's teens grew even closer to them:

- "They are like my second pair of parents."
- "That's our mom and that's our dad. Billy and Katy have been that for us. We got to meet Pastor Billy's own youth pastor and he was like, 'Billy and Katy are out of their minds. They're living with you guys for a month…Billy and Katy are doing this because they want to invest. They aren't just here to be your youth pastor on Wednesdays and Sundays….'"

Let's just put it this way, the youth workers and teenagers at New Life Fellowship in Moline are setting the bar high for what "doing life together" can look like. Billy and Katy are going the extra mile to invest in their teens, and their teens are reaping the benefits of their long-term care.

The authors of *Growing Young* write, "Congregational involvement seems to lessen anxiety by reminding young people of what's important and inviting them to step away from the chaos of their lives to refocus on loving God and others."[5] And the researchers of *Sticky Faith* conclude that "the three things students remember as most significant about youth group are: the adults involved, the community formed and friendships."[6] With so much thought and research behind these topics, it shouldn't surprise us that the teenagers at NLF feel close to their youth leaders, and some of them remain connected long after high school is over.

Imagine being one of Jesus's disciples and spending three years together with him and with each other. They would have known everything about one another. They would have dealt with conflict, loss, sadness, joy, pain, and grief together. They would have seen sides of one another that they'd much rather not deal with. Billy and Katy's group experienced a lot by "doing life together" too. Billy said that the bonds formed over the monthlong Fusion experience have continued on long after the trip was over. I understand, though, that you might not have the time or resources to do life together like Jesus and his disciples did, or to the extent Billy and Katy have—so let's look at some ways to start small.

Start Small

1. Share your story with your teens. Help them get to know the real you, sharing even the really gross parts that you'd much rather not remember (using your discretion, of course).

2. Be the first to share your brokenness. The day I understood this and started practicing it was the day the ministry I was leading started seeing spiritual breakthroughs. My teenagers finally began viewing me not as someone who had it all together, but as someone in need of God's daily grace, just like them.

3. Join teens where they are. They're already at school, so look for ways to spend time with them in that setting. Go to the junior high for lunch once a week. Start a morning prayer group at the high school or get involved in your local Fellowship of Christian Athletes (FCA) or other before-school groups. Volunteer to help coach a sport, or serve as a substitute teacher once a week. Going to all of their ball games, recitals, and events is unrealistic, but seek to engage as many as possible with your time.

4. Be there for them when everything falls apart: encourage, listen, and love. Don't try to fix everything, just be a consistent, loving presence for your teens when things in their lives go wrong.

5. Be very intentional about youth trips. Make sure to remove personal distractions and be fully present for your teenagers. Think of team-building activities and center your conversations around getting to know one another during your time together.

6. Eat meals together. Some of my favorite memories with teens have been formed during these mealtimes.

7. Create space in your youth ministry programming for teenagers to come early and hang out late at youth group. Be ready well in advance so when that one teenager keeps showing up an hour early, you'll be able to be fully present. Understand that it's really not about the program. It's about the relationships being formed.

8. Gather a team of leaders to come alongside you in loving teenagers with their time, energy, and devotion. You can't do it all

alone. The task is too big for just you.

Discipleship on the Fly

A number of years ago I took some teenagers out in our downtown area to write Scripture verses with sidewalk chalk. We thought this would be a good way to encourage people and get them thinking about God. Little did we know, God had something bigger in mind. As we were writing on the sidewalk, we were approached by a young man who claimed to be a Satanist. As you can imagine, we all quickly picked up our sidewalk chalk and joined into a conversation with him. We spent the next hour talking with this man about the truths of Christianity. I was so impressed by some of the things my teenagers said and how they used their knowledge of the Bible to defend their faith. We treated this young man with kindness. We were able to have a respectful discussion about Christianity, and no one raised their voices or became belligerent. This was a moment for me as a youth minister to teach my teens how to share Christ with someone who strongly opposes their beliefs. Had I raised my voice, called this man an idiot, and sent him on his way, I would have done very little for the kingdom—and I would have done an extremely poor job of teaching my teens how to become disciples.

There was another time, though, when I totally blew it. I completely understand what Billy means when he says that your teens see a different side of you during those extended periods together than they do on a typical Sunday or Wednesday. This was cemented for me during a mission trip experience I'd rather not remember. I was struggling internally with the Lord. There was some sin in my life that I wasn't dealing with properly, and so it started dealing with me. On the trip I felt disengaged and to my shame, I spent a lot more time on my phone than I did connecting with my teenagers. My sin kept me from caring for the people in front of me and shut me off from investing in deeper relationships. That trip was very damaging to some of my relationships with the teens in my ministry, and because of my poor attitude and lack of engagement, some of them lost trust in me.

Thankfully, that situation didn't ruin my ability to move forward in ministry. God used that experience to help grow and shape me into a more caring and compassionate leader.

As you can imagine, Billy and Katy have had some not-so-glamorous moments with their teens as well. They told me about one specific trip where everything that could go wrong, did. One year during Fusion they took some teens to Florida for a fun overnight stay on the beach. "It was going to be the highlight of the trip," Billy said. As the group got out and started pitching their tents, they were surrounded by mosquitoes. Billy was still determined that the group was going to spend the night there. "I just decided, we're all a bunch of Northerners, but we are going to push through." As you can imagine, this wasn't a great idea. They hardly slept, and in the morning they were covered in itchy red bites. That day, the group spent about eight hours on the beach. "We only put sunblock on once," Katy admitted, just in the morning. The next day nearly everyone in the group was suffering from massive sunburns. "We all became lobsters," Billy said. "We've got people who are beginning to develop boils on their skin."

"Literally, massive, massive, stupid, ping-pong sized almost," Katy interjected. Billy had gotten in touch with parents to let them know what was going on, and they were, understandably, concerned. Billy and Katy decided to take the group to the health clinic.

On this trip the group was using a borrowed church van. As they pull up to the clinic, "I hear a strange scraping on top of the van, but I'm already going fast enough where I can't stop," Billy said. "It sounded like gunshots!" Katy added.

"I look out the back and there's a massive hole in the ceiling where the hatch used to be," Billy said. "We have a skylight now," Katy joked.

The emergency hatch had caught the low-hanging awning at the clinic. Billy had a fit of anger. "I get out of the vehicle, grab the emergency hatch which is now on the ground, thirty feet behind the vehicle, and I slam it on the ground and I throw a temper tantrum," Billy said. "And it dawns on me in the midst of my tantrum that

I have to keep myself collected to be an example of Jesus in that moment."

"I was trying to keep as level of a head as possible," Katy said. Thankfully, the teenagers were very understanding, and no one guilted Billy for his momentary meltdown.

This is real life, isn't it? As we do life together with the teens in our ministries, we're going to have some not-so-glamorous moments, but thanks to the trust that Billy and Katy had established with their teens prior to the trip, moments like these didn't taint the good work God was doing in and through them on Fusion. That's why it's imperative that you and I approach our roles in youth ministry with grace, love, and humility. Although it was awful for Katy and Billy's group at the time, now it's something they can all laugh about together.

Can you imagine the moments Jesus would have shared with his disciples? I'm sure that messy bunch had their own temper tantrums, but Jesus loved them still. He never asked any of them to stop being his disciples. Disciple-makers walk with others in their mess as they do life together.

As You Are Going

In Matthew 28, Jesus tells us to go and make disciples. In the original language the word "go" means "as you are going." Therefore, as you're running into teens at the football game, "go and make disciples." As you run into traffic on your way to the youth event with a van full of teenagers, "go and make disciples." As you get frustrated in the airport awaiting your flight for the youth mission trip, "go and make disciples."

Don't get too caught up on getting to your destination, whether that's the mission trip location, venue, or sporting event. Make disciples along the way. Be looking for ways to shower teens with the love of Christ and use simple, daily events to teach them how to follow Jesus. We must remember that ministry is not about things, it's about people. It's not about a pat on the back, the praise of man, or a better title. Andrew Root puts it best in his book, *Revisiting Relational Youth Ministry*: "…ministry is about connection, one to another, about sharing in suffering and joy, about persons meeting persons with no pretense or secret motives. It is about shared life, confessing Christ not outside of relationship but within it."[7] The writers of *Sticky Faith* observe that "the average student will learn more about Jesus from the way you greet her when she walks into your youth room and then listen—really listen—as she describes her day, than she will from your wonderful talk about Jesus at the end of the night."[8] The next time you greet a teenager while they're walking through the door, give them your full attention, communicating to them that you really do care about them as a person.

Furthermore, as Root writes,

> We must reach out to their humanity even if it means the suffering of our own humanity, for this is the way of the cross. It may be that the reason they don't trust our offers of friendship is that they intuitively know that we are not willing to see, hear and accompany them in their deepest suffering. We have offered them trips to Disneyland, silly games and "cool" youth rooms, not companionship in their darkest nights, their scariest of hells.[9]

Clark writes that "mid-adolescents generally do not trust adults with the intimate reality of their lives." He goes on to add that "sports, music, dance, drama, Scouts and even faith-related programs are all guilty of ignoring the developmental needs of each individual young person in favor of the organization's goals."[10] I know I have been guilty of allowing numbers to define my success in ministry, and therefore treating teenagers like products to serve my own personal agenda instead of as people to love and care for.

Thankfully, there are great people like Billy and Katy who have walked with teenagers through seasons of deep pain and suffering. Two young people shared with me about how Billy and Katy opened their home to them during times when they had no other safe place to go. Katy and Billy have cried with teenagers and shared their lives with them. They've walked with them into the darkest places of their own personal hells. Thanks to their investment, teenagers' lives are changing, because they know they can come and share their brokenness. In *Adoptive Youth Ministry* Clark writes that "our young desperately need and long for authentic community."[11] The students at NLF found that type of authentic community through their involvement in Fusion.

The youth space at New Life Fellowship is not overly impressive, but what's impressive is the space Billy and Katy have created in their hearts for teenagers. That's what's drawing so many of them into a relationship with Jesus. It's two people who are willing to share their lives with young people and invite them in, especially during their darkest hours.

After all, Jesus models to us that discipleship is best lived out not by telling people what to do, but by showing them how to follow God as we do life together, through deep, authentic relationships. Disciple-makers open doors into their lives for teenagers. Just as Jesus did, they get outside of their comfort zones and get into the messy lives of people who are being shaped into new creations in Christ.

First-Century Youth Ministry

Sabbath Rest

Years ago, I went on a mission trip to India. After returning home I experienced major jet lag. I mean major, I-want-to-crawl-in-a-hole-and-die-because-I-can't-sleep-at-night jet lag. During this period I had a long night of not being able to sleep. The next day I felt absolutely and utterly exhausted. I had youth group that night, so I went home and set my alarm for a short nap. Once my head hit the pillow, I fell asleep quicker than a junior higher loses their registration form for camp. Then somehow, *five hours later* and only thirty minutes before youth group, I woke up. I was so tired I had slept straight through my alarm. Or maybe it went off, and in my exhaustion I shut it off. I really can't remember! My body was so fatigued from my trip that before I could do anything else, I had to get some rest. I was physically tired. It reminds me of something Ruth Haley Barton writes: "Most of us are more tired than we know at the *soul level*. We are teetering on the brink of dangerous exhaustion, and we really cannot do anything until we have gotten some rest."[1]

Together, let's explore the centuries-old practice of the Jewish Sabbath and its implications for our lives today. What does Sabbath have to offer a culture like ours—one that's overly busy, worn out, and in need of rest?

Keeping Up an Exhausting Pace

When I was a kid, I was pretty fast. In junior high my track coach would put me in the 100-meter and 200-meter dash. In those races I always excelled because I got to go at them in a full-out sprint. Then one day my coach put me in the 400-meter dash. I don't know why they call it a "dash"—they should call it the 400-meter "if you try to sprint this as a thirteen-year-old you're going to hit a wall and might pass out." I learned from that experience that in order for me to run that distance well, I had to pace myself. I couldn't go at it in a full-out sprint, otherwise, I'd burn out early and not finish well.

We have to remember that youth ministry is not a sprint. It's a journey, and we must pace ourselves if we're going to stay in the race. The problem is that nearly everything about youth ministry programming is fast-paced. The typical youth ministry calendar is full of fun and exciting opportunities for teenagers: lock-ins, outreach events, mission trips, concerts, camps, and retreats. Add to that the fun and high-energy excitement that happen nearly every time the youth group meets. I wonder, though—could it be that the fast pace is not just hurting us as youth workers, but also hurting our teens?

You'd think with all the fun and excitement available to them teenagers would be feeling great about life, but many teens are not. In his book *Helping the Struggling Adolescent*, Dr. Les Parrott writes that "large scale studies have found that 15 to 20 percent of all adolescents experience painful levels of loneliness."[2] I wonder if the reason they feel so alone is because they've never been taught how to sit still and listen to God, or to be vulnerable before others about their struggles and pain. Could our youth ministry programming actually be stalling growth in our teenagers because we're not creating space and time for rest? In *Hurt 2.0* Chap Clark writes, "we are a culture that has forgotten how to be together."[3] The Sabbath reminds us of the importance of people meeting other people in their own humanity, away from all the busyness and distractions. The practice of Sabbath reminds us to pursue community and to practice stillness together.

For a practicing first-century Jew, everything revolved around the

Sabbath. Their entire week was built around it. Toward the end of the week they centered their time on its preparation. The Sabbath was a day where they ceased their labor to be at rest. There was no need to perform or work hard on the Sabbath. They could simply be human. They could simply be with God.

I do not think it's possible to talk too much about valuing true rest, especially for our youth ministry families. When I run into a youth group family, the first words out of their mouths are very often "we're busy." There's a traveling league to be part of, an event at the school, and a whole host of other things that are vying for their time, energy, and devotion.

Rabbi Abraham Joshua Heschel likens the Sabbath to a pervasive air, a shared space together with the people of God: "The seventh day is like a palace in time with a kingdom for all. It is not a date but an atmosphere."[4] Furthermore, as Heschel beautifully explains, "Six days a week we wrestle with the world, wringing profit from the earth; on the Sabbath we especially care for the seed of eternity planted in the soul. The world has our hands, but our soul belongs to Someone Else."[5] How can an understanding of Sabbath-keeping help revive our souls and teach us about our need for rest?

Come and Be Still

Our culture has lost the art of valuing true rest. We labor about, "working for God," believing that doing and working are what he loves most. Yet, the Sabbath beckons us to come and be present with God and others in a place of rest and enjoyment with our creator and his creation. Jesus says, "'The Sabbath was made for man, not man for the Sabbath'" (Mark 2:27). Since God has planted the seed of his Son into our hearts, how can we grow in our love and adoration of him without rest? No plant will grow without rest, and no Christian will grow without spiritual rest, either.

This is true for us as youth leaders, and for our teenagers and their families. We are called to spend time with God, enjoying him without the pressures of life coming down on us, which can help relieve us from our own prisons of mental, emotional, and physical exhaustion. As the people of God grow, so do our ministries. Discipleship flourishes as disciples learn to sit at the master's feet. Consider the encounter Jesus has with Mary and Martha in the gospels. Martha is busy running about and making preparations, while Mary does nothing but simply sit at the Lord's feet. Jesus lovingly explains to Martha that Mary has chosen what is better. Yes, it is good to work for God, but it is even better to be still before him, to sit at his feet and enjoy fellowship with him. It isn't that Martha chose something bad, it's that what Mary chose is better. The problem is we can't seem to convince ourselves this is true. We place undue pressure on ourselves to perform, and so we keep running, keep moving, keep trying to produce something that seems admirable. Through all of this Jesus beckons us to simply come and be still before him.

I've been there, worn out, tired and exhausted from all the running. I was studying for my master's degree when I read *Sacred Rhythms* by Ruth Haley Barton. This book met me in my personal place of tiredness and exhaustion. As I read I realized my deep need for rest, and I wept after nearly every page. Barton writes, "While our nonstop pace may be tied to genuine passion for what we do (as it was in the disciples' case), we can reach a point where our genuine gifts and passions wear us out because we don't know when to stop."[6] That's where I was when I began my journey toward incorporating more Sabbath into my life. It has been such a joy since then to experience rest and stillness before the Lord. It is truly life-giving and recharging to my soul. Rabbi Heschel writes, "The art of keeping the seventh day is the art of painting on a canvas of time the mysterious grandeur of the climax of creation; as He sanctified the seventh day, so shall we."[7] Sabbath-keeping makes time for us to be refreshed by God, to sit with him in stillness and reflect upon who we are, made in his image. Furthermore, Heschel writes, "It must always be remembered that the Sabbath is not an occasion for diversion of frivolity; not a day to shoot fireworks or turn somersaults, but an opportunity to mend our tattered lives; to connect rather than to dissipate time."[8] The way Heschel writes about the Sabbath makes one truly believe that with Sabbath-keeping comes great delight. The Jewish people even liken the Sabbath to a bride and themselves the groom, ready to receive her.[9] As the observant Sabbath-keeper receives her in all her beauty, he enjoys her company and breathtaking presence.

Keeping the Sabbath

Devout Jews are rigorous in their keeping of the Sabbath. Regarding the religious practice of first-century Jews in *The Feasts of Israel,* Bruce Scott writes, "On Friday night even the humblest dwelling was transformed into a palace of rest and spiritual joy."[10] Devout Jews believe that the Sabbath is something they and God share in common. God gave himself a day of rest, so why shouldn't we? What prevents us from adopting this practice in our own lives?

I would suggest it's that we fear what rest reveals. We fear not doing enough, not becoming someone influential, not keeping up with the rest of the world. We keep moving, believing that our busyness will produce the fruit our fear tempts us to believe will only ripen if we strive constantly for it. Yet no garden grows without the seed being nurtured under the soil, and no heart will produce great fruit for the kingdom unless we allow the master gardener to do his work in it first. Since our rest releases us from the need to always be in control, the enemy will distract us from one of the greatest gifts God has given mankind: the Sabbath, a place in time to simply be human and enjoy fellowship with God, where we cease from our work so that God can work in us instead.

Heschel writes, "The Sabbath is the presence of God in the world, open to the soul of man. God is not in things of space, but in moments of time."[11] In *Between God and Man* Heschel also writes,

> To gain control of the world of space is certainly one of our tasks. The danger begins when in gaining power in the realm of space we forfeit all aspirations in the realm of time. There is a realm of time where the goal is not to have but to be, not to own but to give, not to control but to share, not to subdue but to be in accord. Life goes wrong when the control of space, the acquisition of things of space, becomes our sole concern.[12]

Too much of our time is spent trying to gain dominion over things. We want a vibrant youth ministry, so we seek to control it through our full schedule. We want a stable bank account, so we overwork ourselves to maintain a sense of security. Our teenagers long to be popular, so they spend countless hours trying to perfect their social media presence, hoping for one more follower or "like." We all are constantly giving ourselves over to things, being held captive by them instead of simply learning to be at peace in the presence of God.

Now, I understand that some Jewish people observed the Sabbath to a degree where it became legalistic in its praxis. This is not the kind of Sabbath I'm suggesting we adopt. What I would like to challenge you to explore is what lies at the heart of the Sabbath: rest with God. At its root the word Sabbath means to "cease, desist, to rest."[13] This is the essence of the Jewish practice most needed for us today.

Supporting Families

How can we as youth ministry leaders help stand in the gap for families in our ministries who are overwhelmed by busyness? Since I'm not a parent just yet, I asked my friend Lori, who is a Sabbath-keeping Jewish Christian, if she would share with me about how she and her husband are able to keep the Sabbath in a busy family with six children.

"Heather, it's a matter of priorities," she said, putting it quite simply. "The Sabbath is a gift from God. If you treasure it, you will be blessed by it. It is like a safe haven in a storm."

She describes the Sabbath day for her family like this:

> Our Sabbath is an intentional time of rest. One of my sons says that he looks forward to *Shabbat* because the day is sanctified or set apart from the rest of the week. He says…it makes him think about God. My youngest son says he likes the food especially and the connection to the Jewish practice and the Bible.

For me the *Shabbat* is family connection and a day of reflection on what God has done for us. It is a refreshing time at the end of the week, and it prepares us to go out again when the new week begins.

Sabbath or *Shabbat* celebration in our house goes something like this: On Friday morning I bake bread for the blessing, two loaves of braided *challah*. I clean so the house will be ready for the weekend and I will be able to relax. Also, I begin preparing the evening meal, which always consists of a large dinner and dessert.

Before dusk on Friday we get the table ready with candles and bread and wine/juice and the matches and a little salt. When everyone is at the table, I light the candles and say the blessings over the bread and over the wine. Then dinner is served. We eat and talk and enjoy each other's company.

A Day in the Life

Now, for a little comparison, let's take a look at a day in the life of a typical teenager. We'll call her Chrissy.

Chrissy's alarm goes off at 5:30 a.m. because she's got to get herself to school for show choir practice at 6:30 a.m. After an hour-long practice, she runs to the gas station to grab a slice of breakfast pizza and a Mocha Frappuccino before the school day begins at 7:45 a.m. After a full day of classes, Chrissy quickly changes, inhales a Snickers bar, gulps down a Monster and heads off to volleyball practice. After practice, Chrissy runs home, showers, and heads off to her younger brother's peewee football game. On her way home from the game, Chrissy picks up the pizza her mom called in for dinner. Since it's already 8 p.m. and Chrissy has at least an hour of math homework, instead of sitting down with her family for dinner, she grabs a couple slices of pizza and heads off to her room to tackle the Pythagorean theorem. After she finishes her homework, she starts filling out applications for the scholarships her mom has been pressuring her to apply for. Finally, around 10:30 p.m., Chrissy's head hits the pillow.

The next day she gets up and repeats the same vicious cycle.

If you want to encourage families in your ministry to start incorporating more Sabbath into their lives, consider these things:

1. Teach families the importance of practicing the art of Sabbath. Encourage them to start small, with maybe an afternoon or half a day to begin with if they can't commit to a full day.

2. Ask your senior pastor or teaching pastor to do a series on rest.

3. Instead of taking your teens on a high-energy trip, consider setting up a spiritual retreat for families where they can spend time away from distractions together.

4. Set up time to meet with each family in your youth ministry and listen to how they are doing. Consider walking them through their schedules to see what might be causing them undue stress.

5. Model Sabbath for your teens and families. I have found the best way for me to learn how to do something is by watching someone else do it.

Experiencing God's Power in the Stillness

One of the key elements that helped Jesus's disciples grow and mature in their faith was simply spending time in his presence. There really isn't anything fancy about the way Jesus did discipleship. He simply spent time with people as they did ordinary (and sometimes extraordinary) things, traveling from one small town to the next. As they did life together, free from distractions and the hustle of life, they experienced the power of God.

A few years ago, I experienced the power of God amongst myself and my teens on a week-long mission trip. Time away created an atmosphere for rest and togetherness. Every day we took part in both corporate and private worship, giving us all time to spend with God. We asked that phones be put away and we spent a lot of time together, just talking and sharing about life. As the week went on we became more open and comfortable with one another as authentic conversations flowed.

One night, Mike, one of our leaders, was meeting with his small group of guys. Small group time was supposed to last thirty minutes, but theirs went for nearly two hours. Each time I checked in on the group, I saw the guys huddled around each other in prayer. I couldn't believe what I was seeing. I was humbled and encouraged as the girls and I waited for the guys to come out. When they finally did, the guys were beaming with excitement, thrilled that they had just spent nearly two hours together in prayer. They were on a spiritual high because they had just experienced real fellowship with one another. They opened up to each other, sharing their brokenness, and responded by rallying around each other in prayer.

Then, two days later, something even greater happened. We saw a real revival break out in our group. It was truly amazing. Teenagers were expressing their struggles to one another, and so were the leaders. We were all opening up to each other in a real, honest way, not holding anything back. We spent over four hours together in a room, sharing our lives transparently and praying for each other. There was something about coming together away from outside distractions that brought us closer to God and closer to one another. This week allowed us to taste what Sabbath invites us into, enjoying fellowship with God and others, free from distractions and fully present in a place of rest.

Are our youth ministry calendars creating more busyness and chaos for our teenagers and families, or are they creating the space for families to come, share their burdens, and simply be human? Real rest unveils something good and necessary to understand about our humanity by showing us our need for God's grace, love, and sustaining power. To neglect Sabbath is to ignore something essential. Living without Sabbath is like trying to convince ourselves that we are superhuman—yet we are just people, with limitations, insecurities, and fears. If we don't learn to recognize this in ourselves, we may become depleted, requiring rest we neither planned nor prepared for.

A Tired Soul

As our tired souls look for ways to rest, consider taking the time today to start incorporating more Sabbath into your life. Here are a few suggestions:

1. Set aside a day or an afternoon each week to simply be still before God. Don't put anything on your calendar. Guard it like an important appointment you don't want to miss. I guard my Wednesday mornings and afternoons and keep them free from running around so I can unwind and be present with people and with God.

2. Remove things from your life that cause you unnecessary stress and exhaustion. If something makes you overly anxious, maybe it's because you're not supposed to be doing it right now.

3. Set aside time each day to simply be still before God. This could be five minutes or fifty.

4. Go on a spiritual retreat, where the only tweets you hear come from birds, not from apps on your phone. I've found that the need to constantly be connected to the ministry comes from an unhealthy need in my heart to be in control.

Time with Dad

My earthly father has been a continual presence in my life. Many of my most treasured moments growing up were spent with him. Although my dad and my mom both valued spending time with me and made me feel valued, loved, and important, my father's presence was especially meaningful. It didn't matter what we were doing. We could be watching a Cubs game, throwing the football, or swimming at the pool—all of those experiences were life-giving to me as a child. Little did I realized that our time together was teaching me about who my dad was. I came to understand that he was trustworthy, a man of integrity and immense patience. Although I didn't fully grasp it in childhood, even while splashing around in the pool my dad was teaching me about his character. Thanks to all of my time with him, as an adult I can now see many facets of his character reflected in mine, and for that I am forever grateful.

If we want to make disciples, and if we want to be disciples ourselves, we must be willing to sit at the Lord's feet. Remember, it was Mary who chose what was better. She chose to practice the heart of Sabbath before the feet of the Lord Jesus—to simply be still in his presence. As we start incorporating more Sabbath into our lives, everyone around us will reap the benefits because our lives will be more at peace, content, and full of grace. Heschel writes that the Sabbath invites us to "say farewell to manual work and learn to understand that the world has already been created and will survive without the help of man."[14] It is good to give ourselves the permission to enter into Sabbath. Truly, it is necessary for our souls.

As you consider keeping the Sabbath, start small and invite others on the journey with you. That way, you'll have something valuable to share with each other after a few weeks and months of practicing Sabbath rest.

What I have found is that the best thing I have to share with others is a well-rested, thankful soul that is not burdened down by exhaustion. A heart at rest is a heart that can give fully and freely to others, being completely present with them. That, my friend, is ministry. When we become a safe place for others to land, we invite them into experiencing the quietness of the love that has been rooted deeply into our hearts through time at rest with our Father.

First-Century Youth Ministry

Community-Centered Discipleship

His name was Jose Luis, but everyone called him Cano. I remember the day I met Cano at the church's young adult gathering. You would have thought he'd never encountered a stranger by the way he engaged with every single person. For many months I had been praying for God to bring some real, meaningful friendships into my life. Then along came Cano and a great group of young adults.

Every week Cano would get all of us young adults together for a social activity. We'd have dinner at someone's home, go out for ice cream, catch a show in the downtown area, or meet up somewhere after Bible study. I miss those days of constant, refreshing community, of sharing our lives together, serving with one another, and enjoying fellowship around the table. I miss playing games, singing, praying, and fasting for one another in times of spiritual crisis. My time spent with this group was one of the most life-giving periods of my life because we were forming a community where we cared for, supported, and truly loved one another. We walked with each other through divorce, seasons of loss, marriages, and celebrations. As we grew in our love for God and for one another, we were truly experiencing in some small way what the early church did in the book of Acts:

They devoted themselves to the apostles' teaching and to

> fellowship, to the breaking of bread and to prayer. Everyone was
> filled with awe at the many wonders and signs performed by
> the apostles. All the believers were together and had everything
> in common. They sold property and possessions to give to
> anyone who had need. Every day they continued to meet
> together in the temple courts. They broke bread in their homes
> and ate together with glad and sincere hearts, praising God
> and enjoying the favor of all the people. And the Lord added to
> their number daily those who were being saved. (Acts 2:42-47)

Have you ever stopped to contemplate the fact that the early
church, described here in Acts, would have been a primarily Jewish
community of believers?[1] It's likely that for them living in community
wasn't so hard because it was just part of who they were as a people.
Community was rooted deeply into their DNA. I asked my Jewish
friend Lori to help me better understand just how important
community is in the Jewish world. She said, "Heather, it's deeply
embedded within the entire scope of Judaism. It's just something
that's assumed. No one really thinks that much about it, because of
how deeply embedded it is in our understanding of who we are."
In "The Importance of Community (Kehilla) in Judaism," Rabbi
Jill Jacobs writes, "membership in a Jewish community has always
demanded a sense of shared destiny, manifested in the obligation
to care for other members of the community, as well as in the joy
of partaking in others' celebrations."[2] We see all of this lived out in
the early church. A sense of belonging, a shared destiny, and the
responsibility to care for one another. Do we see these same aspects
lived out in our youth ministry communities?

"We" Not "Me"

Lois Tverberg argues that some of the reason why we lack a true
understanding of community in our Western world is because we
read the Bible with "me" language instead of "we" language. She
observes that "English speakers have a habit of reading every 'you'
in the Bible as if it's addressed to 'me all by myself' rather than 'me
within God's larger community.'"[3] God spoke to Moses, but for the
benefit of the entire community of Israel. He spoke to the prophets,

but again, all for the purpose of engaging the entire community of Israel. It was a message in time, not just for the individual, but for the collective people of God.

For an example of this, let's take a look at the biblical story of Achan. Achan is a man who took for himself things that were plundered from the land of Canaan—things that Israel was commanded not to take from the temple. As the story goes in the book of Joshua, "But the Israelites were unfaithful in regard to the devoted things; Achan son of Karmi, the son of Zimri, the son of Zerah, of the tribe of Judah, took some of them. So, the Lord's anger burned against Israel" (Joshua 7:1).

If you notice, God's righteous anger didn't burn toward Achan, his anger burned toward Israel. But why? Wasn't Achan the one sinning? To help us fully grasp what's going on here we have to step into the shoes of someone from the Middle East. There was an understanding within this community that everyone had a responsibility to one another. Jacobs writes that in Judaism, "a community must provide for all of its members' spiritual and physical needs."[4] Achan's sin wasn't just his, it was the community's, because the community had a responsibility to Achan, just as Achan had a responsibility to his community.

The book of James encourages us in a similar manner: "My brothers and sisters, if one of you should wander from the truth and someone should bring that person back, remember this: Whoever turns a sinner from the error of their way will save them from death and cover over a multitude of sins" (James 5:20). Weaved throughout the entire Bible is a continual focus on the importance of community and the responsibility we have to one another. (Other passages to look at on this subject: Hebrews 10:24-25, Galatians 6:2, 1 Corinthians 12:25-27, Genesis 2:18, Ecclesiastes 4:9-12.)

Becoming a Team

Years ago in high school, my girls' basketball team had to end practice with all twenty-plus of us making two free throws each. If an individual missed her free throws we had to run down and backs across the court together as a team. We kept doing this until everyone had made her free throws. There were a couple of girls who just couldn't get the ball in the hoop, so we kept running and running and running some more. It wasn't just the two girls who were being punished; we all suffered for it. There was an understanding that we were a team and because we were a team, we suffered together.

This mentality is especially evident in the book of Acts when the early church is forming. This group of Jewish believers starts turning their little place in the world upside down because of their love for God and for one another. It wasn't so much what they did, built, or accomplished that drew others to want to join in their company, it was how they acted and received one another in love and faith. The members of the early church were truly a team.

Your youth ministry is a team, too. Our teams have a responsibility to love each other, provide for one another, and hold each other accountable. There's a girl in my former ministry whose family couldn't afford new clothes, so we took her shopping and bought her brand-new clothes. When another teenager suffered a health crisis we spent time with him in the hospital while he was recovering. There have also been those times when teenagers needed to be held accountable, and so loving conversations have taken place. Without love, care, concern, and accountability, your youth ministry will struggle to grow into a vibrant community.

The other day I was officiating a basketball game for two teams on opposite ends of the talent spectrum. "Well, this should be a pretty boring game. It's most likely going to be a blow out," I said to the second official before the game. By all accounts, it started that way, but then something happened. There was a shift in the momentum as the underdog team hit a few good shots. We saw them start to come together. There was energy, belief, and excitement. The other team began crumbling from within. You could see the fear and doubt on their faces. As their team fell apart, the underdogs stepped right up, and before you knew it, we had ourselves a ball game. The underdog team ended up winning by two points in overtime. When the buzzer sounded, there was a roar of excitement from the winning team so loud it felt like they had won the Super Bowl, not a Friday night JV basketball game. Together they accomplished something no one thought they could.

Many of our youth ministries are struggling to make disciples because we're not becoming a team. We're not supporting one another in love. We're not valuing others above ourselves. We're not cheering one another on to overcome adversity. We're self-focused and not others-focused. We're concerned about our own agenda for youth ministry and what we think it's supposed to be, rather than simply focusing on having it be a place where teenagers can grow together in a community where they're deeply loved.

Imagine yourself as the captain of your youth ministry team with Jesus as your coach. Jesus has entrusted the health of the team to you. How healthy is your team?

Discipleship Around the Table

I heard something interesting on the radio the other day. A gentleman was arguing that the symbol that represents Jesus's life best is not the cross, but a table. His reasoning was that Jesus was constantly inviting people to join in fellowship with him, most commonly around a table. Tverberg and Spangler observe,

> though the Israelites didn't have fancy tables or place settings, they had something better. For them, the table was much more than a place to eat. It was a place of mutual trust and vulnerability. Sitting down at the same table with someone meant that you shared a protected relationship with them.[5]

Growing up Baptist, I often found myself sitting around a table enjoying a potluck meal with my church congregation. Someone once said to me that a good Baptist comes to church with a Bible in one hand and a spoon in the other. It was a running joke within our congregation that Baptists love to eat. As a child I enjoyed many, many potlucks with my church family, along with other celebrations around a table that brought us together. In these moments friendships grew, laughter was shared, and life became more sacred. Around the table we became more than just acquaintances in a crowd, but friends who shared life together.

Barry Jones puts it beautifully:

> Tables are one of the most important places of human connection. We're often most fully alive to life when sharing a meal around a table. We shouldn't be surprised, then, to find that throughout the Bible God has a way of showing up at tables. In fact, it's worth noting that at the center of the spiritual lives of God's people in both the Old and New Testaments, we find a table: the table of Passover and the table of Communion.[6]

In Jewish culture, the table was a place of fellowship and connection. In "Understanding Jewish Meals in Their Context," Dr. Eli Lizorkin-Eyzenberg writes, "sharing meals often expresses the universal Near Eastern value of hospitality."[7] The Jewish people see a meal as more than an opportunity to shove down a Hot Pocket before everyone quickly runs off to their next activity. They see it as something deeply spiritual. As Lizorkin-Eyzenberg also writes, "in the East all aspects of life are perceived as spiritual occasions and when it comes to meals the kitchen table and the altar are inseparable."[8]

Let's take a moment to think long and hard about our student ministries. How much of what we do centers around a table? Around the table, we share life, enjoy a meal, laugh together, and grow in our understanding of one another through deep, meaningful conversation. We cry, rejoice, pray, and sing around a table. We sit and still ourselves before the Lord and one another (as long as no one is glued to their smartphone).

One of the last things Jesus does before he goes to the cross is join in a meal around a table with his disciples. Then, before Jesus ascends back into heaven, he enjoys a breakfast of grilled fish on the Sea of Galilee with a few of those disciples. It's no surprise, then, that the crescendo of Jesus's returning is a wedding banquet. Obviously, time around the table means something to Jesus.

During my time in Israel I played on a women's basketball team based in Jerusalem, and out of that I naturally built some deeper bonds with the women on my team. John gave us some advice: "If one of your teammates invites you to their home for a meal, you CANNOT refuse it. You must go. If you refuse, it is like a gigantic, disrespectful slap in the face." John told us that in the Middle Eastern world, a shared meal is extremely significant because it indicates a meaningful bond of friendship between two parties. We were not allowed to say no (and we were also told that we had to eat everything on our plates as well—otherwise, we would deeply offend the family). Placing value on life around the table can have a deep impact on our culture and our relationships—and can also have a deep impact on our ministries.

What Teenagers Want Most

Go ahead, take the temperature of your youth ministry community. Is it inviting, or do teenagers feel like you're one of the coldest spots in town? In her book *Thriving Youth Groups*, longtime youth worker and youth ministry coach Jeanne Mayo comments on a survey in *Group* magazine about what young people are most looking for in a youth ministry. She writes, "The highest ratings in the 'very important' category were the following:

1. A welcoming atmosphere where you can be yourself—73 percent
2. Quality relationships with other teenagers—70 percent"[9]

Teenagers are longing for and looking for community. The writers of *Growing Young* found that one key component of churches that are attracting and keeping young people is something they termed a "warmth cluster":

> In our analyses of the terms young people and adults use to describe their own churches or parishes, we noticed repeated words such as welcoming, accepting, belonging, authentic, hospitable, and caring. We began to call this the warmth cluster.

Across the board in statistical analyses, the warmth cluster emerged as a stronger variable than any one program. And while 6 out of 10 interviewees mentioned group practices like small groups, youth group, and retreats when they talked about why their church is thriving, what seems important about those practices is that they create space for young people to be together and nurture relationships.[10]

All people, no matter what age, are looking for a place to belong, and a place to receive comfort and support. Every teen is looking for a place where they can share their burdens without being looked down on or pushed aside because of their brokenness and struggles.

Orion stepped into our youth ministry as a teen, when he was looking for authentic community. He shared with a group of us how important it was that we knew his name. He said that just knowing that others knew his name made him feel welcomed and like he belonged. Another teenager, Trenton, was talking about his experience at youth group when he said, "Before I went to this group I didn't really feel happy. I always felt like I was lonely and that no one really cared. When I joined Collide, Jesus showed me that he cares. Everyone here cares that I'm not lonely." I know you have stories like Orion's and Trenton's in your ministry, too. These are the stories we should be celebrating: stories of teenagers finding the love of God in a community of Christians who have embraced them in all of their messiness. As the authors of *Growing Young* put it,

> The warmth young people seek isn't usually clean and tidy. That's just fine, because family isn't neat. It's messy. And *messy* is a good word to describe what young people want from a congregation. They desire not only to share their own messiness but also walk alongside the authentic messiness of others.[11]

Frog-Kissing

Remember Billy and Katy from chapter five? They embraced teens with messy lives and welcomed them into their homes. Community is not going to look neat. It's going to bring you lots of headaches and make you question if it's really worth it. Yet there are hearts behind each person in your youth ministry, and each of those people needs something real, authentic, and lasting. Jeanne Mayo writes that her method of creating an atmosphere where kids can come and be as they are is to become what she terms a professional frog-kisser:

> What's the kiss? The magical transformation in your teenagers will come after you, your adult leaders, or your students, in the name of Christ's love, offer them the kiss of encouragement. You choose to look past the warty junk on the outside and discover the incredible things that are always—*always*—somewhere hidden on the inside.[12]

Jesus was a professional frog-kisser too. He kissed the "warty faces" of prostitutes, sinners, and lepers. He welcomed the most wretched people in town to come and join his community. He welcomed them with open arms. Even some of the disciples were a little warty. As Mayo puts it, "Simon had a lot of potential and Jesus knew it… Christ's response to Simon's froggish conduct was something a little unexpected. *Jesus changed his name.* He believed in Peter."[13]

Bring Community to Your Life and Ministry

If you're ready for this kind of community, consider the following.

1. As Mayo writes, "We teach what we know, but we reproduce who we are."[14] If you want to build community, you must have a heart that is welcoming, open, and inviting. You can't fake it. If you're not there yet, ask God to grow your heart in love and compassion.

2. Read the book *Thriving Youth Groups* by Jeanne Mayo.

3. Start serving the downtrodden. Look for ways to engage the teenagers in your community who are lost and lonely.

4. Get down on their level. You can't create community if you want to be the king or queen of your youth ministry. Jesus humbled himself and became a human being. We too must

humble ourselves and get down on the level of our teens, putting ourselves on an equal playing field.

5. Start kissing some frogs. Make teens feel treasured, valued, and cared for by going out of your way to encourage them.

6. Look for opportunities to spend time with teenagers around a table. Eat meals, sing, pray, and study God's Word together.

7. Create a warm, inviting atmosphere by breaking down cliques.

Abraham's Seed

From Abraham's seed, God would birth a community of people, the community of Israel. This community would be distinctly different and set apart from the rest of the world. There's a seed God wants to plant in our youth ministries too—a seed of his transforming love that goes beyond cliques, coolness, and trying to be someone we're not. This transforming love says, "Come as you are, with all your baggage, your froggy warts, and your brokenness, and receive the love of God through the grace and forgiveness of the cross. Come be part of our community, no matter what your background, social status, or coolness factor."

Seeds like this take time to nurture. Don't expect community to happen overnight. It could take months or maybe even years to see a true change in the culture of your youth ministry, depending on the current state. Yet, it was love that changed the world. It was love that endured, suffered, and died on Calvary so that we could come and sit at Jesus's table and enjoy fellowship with him. I imagine it was love that drove Cano to pull all of us together and pioneer a thriving community of young adults who supported and cared for one another. There has to be love in our hearts if we're going to form a community where teenagers can come and be changed by Jesus. Only love can move beyond a Wednesday night service and into the lives of a community of teenagers and families for the glory of God.

Kung Fu Discipleship

Do you remember the remake of the movie *The Karate Kid*? I'm talking about the 2010 release with Jaden Smith playing Dre Parker. Young Dre finds himself in a bit of trouble after school when some bullies make him their target. Mr. Hahn, played by Jackie Chan, comes to Dre's rescue by using his kung fu skills and Dre is hooked. He wants to know kung fu like Mr. Hahn does and so he becomes his apprentice. The two spend many, many hours training together, and along the way Mr. Hahn teaches Dre quite a few life lessons.[1]

As part of Dre's training, a technique is used in which Dre and Mr. Hahn stand facing each other with two bamboo poles tied to their wrists. Each holds opposite ends of the poles, linking them to one another. As the two of them move together with the bamboo poles, Dre mimics his teacher's movements, learning to fight like him as he follows his master.

There are many young people looking for someone like Mr. Hahn to invest in their lives, someone who's willing to lead them toward truth, serving as a master disciple of God's Word for them and pointing them to the true master, Jesus Christ. Teenagers are longing for relationships that are real and authentic. Most of the time teens don't feel like they can truly be themselves. They're always wondering,

"Will this person accept me?" and "Can I trust this person to love me for who I really am?" Usually, the answer they tell themselves is no, so they try to be someone they're not in the hopes of getting people to like them.

In the church, mentoring relationships offer young people an opportunity to be and become their true selves, children made in the image of God. Mentoring relationships give them a chance to share their brokenness and be received with love, growing into something brand new as they journey together with trusted mentors toward the transformative love of God. Root includes these words from a youth pastor in *Revisiting Relational Youth Ministry*: "I'm convinced if they're going to follow Jesus in college and the rest of their lives, it will be because they had a relationship with one another and with somebody older who modeled that."[2]

Discipleship as Apprenticeship

Although you won't find the word mentor in the Bible, mentorship is practiced all throughout the Scriptures. The word *mentor* actually comes from Homer's *Odyssey*; Mentor was an older friend of Odysseus. He helped guide and raise Telemachus, Odysseus's son, while Odysseus was away from home fighting the Trojan War.[3] There are many teens growing up in homes where life is a little chaotic, where maybe one or both parents is absent physically, emotionally, or spiritually. Even teenagers growing up in Christian homes would benefit from a mentor. I'm not saying we should replace parents as the key disciple-makers of their children, but simply that we should come alongside parents to help in the difficult years of raising teenagers.

Youth ministry research shows that teens are longing for mentors, people to extend God's love, showing them that they care and are invested in their lives. The writers of *Growing Young* draw out wisdom from theologian Miroslav Volf, who puts it this way: "'We are the church' doesn't mean, 'We meet occasionally' or 'We cooperate in a current project.' Instead, *we actually become part of one another*."[4] In his book *Blur*, Jeff Keuss, a professor of Christian ministry, theology, and culture, notes that teenagers have "a deep hunger to connect with others and discover the grace found in other people through these relationships."[5] And in his research, Chap Clark has found that "young people are desperate for an adult who cares."[6] It's obvious that teenagers are looking for adults who will show them genuine love and concern, and a mentor can help fill those gaps. We can adhere to the wisdom of the Jewish sages: "Make for yourself a mentor, acquire for yourself a friend."[7]

Acquire for Yourself a Mentor

Mentorship really isn't all that complicated. I've sought out many who, at the time, probably weren't even aware they were playing the role of a mentor in my life. They were simply passing the things they loved on to me. My dad taught me how to play softball and basketball. Travis was the person I sought out in college to help refine my golf game. Guys like Joe, Rocky, and Mike have all helped me become a better basketball official. My mom taught me how to cook and bake. Susan taught me how to really listen and care for hurting people. Jeanne taught me how to be a strong, confident, courageous, and capable leader in youth ministry. John started me on the path of understanding Jesus in the context of his Jewish culture, and he's the one I go to when I have questions about the Jewish roots of our faith. All of these people had something I desired but didn't possess: knowledge and wisdom from years of experience and learning. In many ways, I apprenticed myself to them with the hopes of becoming like them.

An apprentice is someone who "is learning by practical experience under skilled workers a trade or calling."[8] Understanding the apprentice-discipleship model is key to understanding how Jesus did discipleship. In his article *Discipleship, What Is It?* Joshua Moss writes,

> ...the disciple was like the rabbi's "apprentice." Just as an apprentice carpenter would observe, learn from, and imitate the master carpenter until he could make tables, plows, and other items with equal precision and excellence, the rabbinic disciples were to observe, imitate, and study all their rabbi's ways, that they, too, might become masters of the Word of God,

able to handle it with equal skill and compassion.[9]

Tverberg and Spangler shed light on the apprenticeship model of discipleship in *Sitting at the Feet of Rabbi Jesus* when they write about the relationship between Elijah and Elisha: "Where did the rabbis develop their ideas of discipleship? They found their model in Scripture, especially in the relationship of two men—the prophets Elijah and Elisha."[10] Furthermore, Tverberg and Spangler go on to add, "Like any disciple, Elisha's goal was not just to study from Elijah, but to become *like* Elijah in order to carry on his ministry as a prophet to Israel.[11]

1 Kings 19:19-21 tells the story:

> So Elijah went from there and found Elisha son of Shaphat. He was plowing with twelve yoke of oxen, and he himself was driving the twelfth pair. Elijah went up to him and threw his cloak around him. Elisha then left his oxen and ran after Elijah. "Let me kiss my father and mother goodbye," he said, "and then I will come with you."
>
> "Go back," Elijah replied. "What have I done to you?"
>
> So Elisha left him and went back. He took his yoke of oxen and slaughtered them. He burned the plowing equipment to cook the meat and gave it to the people, and they ate. Then he set out to follow Elijah and became his servant.

With its strange twist of events, this encounter between Elijah and Elisha seems odd to our Western thinking. What's up with the cloak? Why is Elisha so quick to leave everything, even doing away with his own livestock and farming equipment in the process?

Elijah was well-known in Israel as a prophet of God. Elijah would have been the model to follow for any man who desired to know God and be active in service for him during that time. By throwing his cloak (mantle) around Elisha, Elijah communicates something more than just trying to keep Elisha's shoulders warm from the breeze. As one commentary puts it, "This was an investiture with the prophetic office. It is in this way that the Brahmins, the Persian Sufis, and other priestly or sacred characters in the East are appointed."[12] In a stunning scene, Elijah was communicating to Elisha that he was appointing him to the prophetic office! It's no wonder Elisha dropped everything to follow after Elijah, becoming his apprentice.

The time Elijah invested into Elisha must have paid some major dividends, because in the end, Elisha gets a double portion of Elijah's spirit and does twice as many miracles as him. Isn't that the point of mentorship, to help others do even greater things than you?

One of the pastors at my church is awesome at this. Just like Elijah, Pastor Brandon has something that attracts others to him and makes them want to be like him. As the worship arts pastor he is constantly investing in people with musical talent and raising them up to lead. There's one teen girl, Faith, he's working with right now whose heart is coming to life as she sees that Pastor Brandon is valuing her gift, helping her grow in it, and giving her the opportunity to use it. My guess is Pastor Brandon has asked the Lord to multiply his life and help him make people even better than he is at leading others in worship to God. I can only hope that through Brandon's investment in Faith, she'll receive a double blessing from God just like Elisha.

How can you be like Elijah? Start by investing your life in someone, caring for their growth and looking to give them leadership opportunities. After all, when it comes down to it we're all just interim youth pastors, aren't we? Therefore, we should always be seeking to train up our replacement, like Elijah did with Elisha, so that when the time comes we can pass the baton to them, either to take our place or lead in a different context. Jesus's call to make disciples is one of multiplication. May we seek to multiply ourselves in ways that help others grow and increase the kingdom of God.

Paul and Timothy

We also see the apprenticeship model lived out between Paul and Timothy. Timothy was a recent convert to Christianity who lived in

Lystra; his father was Greek and his mother was Jewish. He and Paul became acquainted with one another on one of Paul's missionary journeys. From what we can tell, there was an instant bond between the two and a mentoring relationship was formed. Alton Chua and Pelham Lessing observe four dynamics that were true of Paul and Timothy's relationship:

1. Attraction: The mentor must see the potential value in working with the protégé, while the protégé must look up to the mentor as a model.

2. Relationship: A strong relationship is necessary for mentoring to be impactful.

3. Responsiveness: For spiritual growth and maturity to take place, the protégé needs to be teachable, submissive, and responsive to the direction of the mentor.

4. Accountability: The mentor is responsible for evaluating how the protégé progresses, and holding the protégé accountable along the path for growth.[13]

Chua and Lessing observe that Paul's main actions with Timothy were empowerment and deployment.[14] Paul invested in Timothy, took him along on missionary journeys, wrote to him, and prayed for him, acting as a continual presence in Timothy's life. Paul shows genuine love and concern for Timothy, even referring to him as "my dear son" (2 Timothy 1:2), serving with Timothy in the work of the gospel (Philippians 2:22), and reminding Timothy to hold fast to the faith and preserve sound doctrine (2 Timothy 1:13). It's obvious that Paul and Timothy had a very strong relationship with each other. As Dr. Annita D'Amico and Dr. René Rochester write, "discipleship and apprenticeship are deeply rooted in relationships."[15] Paul was able to pass on to Timothy something more valuable than just information: his life's work and his passion, which, in turn, became Timothy's passion too.

Much of Paul and Timothy's mentoring relationship centered around doing ministry together, as it did with Elijah and Elisha and with Jesus and his disciples. Spangler and Tverberg observe, "The disciple would accompany the rabbi on all of his daily rounds: going to court, helping the poor, burying the dead, redeeming slaves, and so on."[16] Even the smallest ministry tasks were shared by a rabbi and their disciple.

Mentorship is multifaceted. It's not linear. Mentorship goes beyond the classroom and into our lives. A mentor takes their apprentice past the pages of a book and into the halls of their own hearts. Mentors share their lives with those they mentor—their hurts, pains, joys, and stories of redemption. A mentor listens with the intent not to fix, but to care for their apprentice. Each moment in time when a mentor and apprentice share space, an opportunity arises for the two to grow in their love and care for one another as persons being made in the image of God. Although doing ministry together is an important piece of mentorship, it isn't everything. I have found that some of my best conversations about life with teenagers happened not when we were studying the Bible, but when we were cooking together, going for a walk, or working on a project.

Meet Jeanne and Cassidy

Years ago, I was mentoring a bright teenage girl named Cassidy. One day, the Lord spoke to me that I was supposed to pass her off to another woman in the church. When I brought it up to Cassidy she was in full agreement. Jeanne and Cassidy have been meeting for the past three and a half years, and although there is a fifty-year age gap between the two of them, it's made no difference. Jeanne, a sixty-seven-year-old retired teacher, has poured her life into Cassidy, now a seventeen-year-old senior in high school. Their mentoring relationship has proven meaningful and life-changing for both of them. I thought they might have a thing or two to teach us about what mentoring relationships between a teenager and an older adult could look like in the church, so I sat down with them not long ago to ask some questions.

Jeanne started off the conversation. "Even with the age disparity, I can still speak some truth into her life, which gives me a sense of worth," she said. "And, also just to see her perspective and to see how much she loves the Lord, it just lifts my spirit. Because she's on fire for the Lord and that's just so awesome to see…I'm sure I have gained as much from her as she has from me." "Since Jeanne came into my life I have grown so much in my faith," Cassidy said. "And seeing someone who has been through so much and has had so many years beyond me I am able to think about how I can take what she has taught me into the future and into my relationship with the Lord. And it's just been so awesome to see how we mesh so well and how conversations just flow." Cassidy even wrote a paper about Jeanne because Jeanne is who comes to mind when she thinks of the term "Christian woman."

Cassidy said Jeanne has taught her a lot: "Putting others before yourself, being humble with the Lord, humility and giving…because [Jeanne] does that daily in her walk with the Lord," she said. Jeanne has been encouraged by Cassidy's faith too. "I think I see in her what I wish I would have been at her age," Jeanne said. "She just has that confidence in [Jesus] that allows her to speak that truth into others' lives. She has a boldness that I don't have in that way and wish I did, so it kind of spurs me on that if she can do it at that age, I can do it at this age."

Their relationship has grown to the point where Cassidy will come over to Jeanne's house after school just to do homework or hang out before she goes on to her next activity for the evening. "My home is open to her," Jeanne said. Jeanne not only helps guide Cassidy spiritually, speaking wisdom and grace into her life, but she even helps her with English papers. "Even when we are writing or typing, that's been good bonding for sure," said Cassidy.

They've walked through books like *Lies Women Believe* and listened to messages on body image, but the majority of the time they simply talk about what's going on in Cassidy's life. "We just talk about situations…and it's been me listening and sometimes offering some words of wisdom," said Jeanne.

"Yes, and we always end in prayer," Cassidy quickly added.

I asked Jeanne what she would say to an adult who might feel too old to mentor a teenager. Her advice? "Just give it a try, because when you first asked me, I thought, *Can I still relate?* But, I think it's like anything else—you will never know until you try, and now there's a connection I could have never even dreamed of."

"Kids my age might be skeptical about it too," Cassidy said. "However, until they give it a try also they wouldn't realize the wisdom those people do have and that their age honestly doesn't make a difference."

Both of them expressed how deeply meaningful this mentoring relationship has been and how much they are going to miss one another once Cassidy leaves for college. "This has been one of the most meaningful relationships in my high school career," Cassidy said at the end of our conversation.

The bond that's been formed between Jeanne and Cassidy is something special. Relationships like this shouldn't be rare in the church, but commonplace. If two people are willing to open their lives to one another, bonds like this can become the norm. Consider sharing Jeanne and Cassidy's story with people in your congregation who are interested in becoming a mentor for a young person.

Starting Your Own Mentorship Ministry

The goal of mentorship is not to create another program for teenagers to get involved in, but for them to experience, through us, what it's like to be an apprentice of the Lord Jesus Christ. When we invite teens deep into our lives, things like the joy of Christ and the wisdom of God that have grown in us through years of maturity serve as lighthouses for our teenagers. Now teens see that, yes indeed, Rabbi Jesus is alive and active. The fire for God in our souls becomes a spark that lights a fire in their hearts to be passionate disciples of Rabbi Jesus. As we care for, instruct, counsel, and lovingly rebuke those we mentor, we grow not a program but people. And as the people of God grow, so does the kingdom.

Maybe you're ready to be a mentor or start a mentoring program at your church. As always, it's good to be reminded that discipleship is messy, so don't be surprised if the journey feels a little rocky—that's inevitable, but don't give up on the process. Whenever our lives become entangled with someone else's, there's always going to be a growing process as we learn to trust one another.

Key Components of Starting Your Own Mentorship Ministry

As you consider starting a mentoring ministry, here are some helpful tips:

1. Gather maturing Christian adults who are willing to walk alongside young people.
2. Train your adult leaders on how to mentor someone.

   Consider covering the following components in your training:

   - Establish trust with your mentee by showing them that you truly care.

   - Be appropriately honest and open about your own struggles with your mentee.

   - Consider keeping it light before you dive in too deep. Maybe asking your mentee about their deepest, darkest secrets isn't the avenue to take right away. Give the relationship time to grow and seek the Holy Spirit's wisdom.

   - Choose a book of the Bible to study together.

   - Find something you share in common and go and experience that together.

   - Consider teaching your mentee something you know more about that they have an interest in (like fixing cars, fishing, sewing, cooking, playing the guitar, etc.).

   - Prepare your mentee to serve in some capacity in ministry by setting goals for them. When they're ready, propel them forth with the opportunity to lead.

   - Pray, encourage, and lovingly rebuke your mentee.

   - Meet at least once a month, preferably two or three times per month.

- Invite your mentee into your life: Have them over for dinner, let them see how you parent, how you do marriage, or how you interact with others.

3. Follow up with your adult mentors every couple of months to see how things are going. Offer them any support or encouragement they might need.

4. Remind your adult mentors that mentoring is going to be messy, teenagers are probably going to be flaky at times, and it will sometimes be discouraging and frustrating. Encourage them to persevere.

5. Consider setting up a covenant for the mentor and mentee to sign as they make a commitment to their mentoring relationship.

6. Ask mentors to make a one-year commitment (at minimum). Lord willing, the relationship will continue on after that first year!

7. Start small, and don't overwhelm yourself by trying to pick a mentor for every single teenager. Meet with teens and parents to see who's interested and who would follow through with the commitment.

8. Evaluate, reevaluate, and reevaluate some more! It's going to be a growing process, but don't give up. It will be worth it!

Grow the Kingdom Through Mentorship

Our teens can change the world if we are willing to come alongside them and fan into flame the gift of God that the Lord Jesus has placed inside of them. As we share life, including some of the messy and gross parts, we can grow together in Christ—not because we have it all together, but because we're willing to admit that we don't. When we get to that place of authentic relationship, we're no longer acting as pious leaders, but as loving mentors who point teens to the one who does have it together—Jesus. As we grow together like Elijah and Elisha, care for one another like Jeanne and Cassidy, and pursue God together like Paul and Timothy, disciples are made, the kingdom increases, and the world is forever changed.

First-Century Youth Ministry

Church as Family

My friend Zac has a leader in his youth ministry who is ninety-three years old. Zac says Ray is his teens' most-loved volunteer because "they can feel his heart for them." Ray is always "offering hugs, words of encouragement, and support," Zac says. The teenagers in Zac's ministry know Ray really cares.

I had the privilege of sitting down with Zac and Ray to ask them what having a guy like Ray has brought to Zac's youth ministry. "I was about seventy years old when I started out in youth ministry and have loved it ever since," Ray said. That's right—Ray started out in youth ministry in 1996 at the age of seventy. It all began when the youth pastor at his church resigned. Ray and another gentleman stepped up to lead the youth ministry during the interim period.

"There's so much energy [in teenagers] that if we can put that energy to the Lord we could accomplish so much," Ray said of what he loves about working with teens. Ray added that working with teenagers offers him a purpose. "One of the most wonderful blessings of my life at this point is being able to go to youth group and interact with those young people."

I asked Zac if Ray's age held him back in any way. "Yes and no," Zac said. "Yes, because he doesn't understand what we're talking about sometimes because of youth culture; and no, because he's all about relationships and he knows how to love people well. He's able to work through the barrier of not understanding everything about youth culture and have a relationship with the students in spite of it, because he's relational and he loves them. The relationship matters more than what he doesn't understand culturally."

As a leader, Zac says that Ray has taught him about the power of prayer. He often finds Ray praying over teens without hesitation. This is something the teenagers love; they know that Ray will stop at a moment's notice to lift up their needs before the Lord. Zac said that even though there are other leaders who are closer in age to the teenagers and might be more relatable, "Ray is more loved by the students because Ray doesn't have all the distractions a young person with kids might have. So, when he's there, he's really focused on being there, and the students can feel that." Zac said this has helped Ray serve as a great mentor for teens. "He has the time to really disciple them."

I asked Ray what he would say to older congregation members who might be hesitant to get involved in youth ministry. "Those kids are so open and so hungry for someone to come alongside of them. Seventy-some years since I was a high school student, things aren't that much different," (other than smartphones) he said.

"Age has not been a hindrance, because they see that I'm interested in them," Ray said. Teenagers are hungry for meaningful relationships, and Ray's words remind us that no one is too old to care for another human being.

Every week Ray brings 3 x 5 cards with him to youth group. He asks every teenager he encounters how he can pray for them and writes it down on the cards. Then he takes those cards home and prays over all of those requests. Ray told me that "students trust me, because they know that I'm praying for them." Ray follows up with teens, showing that he really does genuinely care. "I want to show kids they are worth something," Ray said.

If you're ready to start incorporating older generations into your youth ministry you'll likely encounter obstacles in the form of the words, "I'm too old for this." But, your youth ministry needs people like Ray who can serve as spiritual grandparents in the faith. Keep sending the message to your older congregation members that the youth ministry *needs them.* Consider sharing Ray's experience as you invite older folks within your congregation to come alongside your teenagers as you unite the generations.

A Jewish Perception of the Aged

The Jewish people highly valued the older generations. In *Our Father Abraham*, Marv Wilson writes, "the Hebrew Scriptures assert that the pinnacle of a person's life is old age." He adds, "A midrash states, 'One who takes advice from elders never stumbles.'"[1] It goes without saying that young people need to be surrounded by the wisdom of other generations as they grow to be disciples. Job even begs the question, "Is not wisdom found among the aged? Does not long life bring understanding?" (Job 12:12). Teenagers need the wisdom of not just their own grandparents and family elders, but an extended family of giants in the faith, those who've walked this journey much longer than they have. We as youth workers need that wisdom too.

Wilson comments, "With gray hair came respect and honor: 'Rise in the presence of the aged, show respect for the elderly and revere your God. I am the LORD' (Lev. 19:32). In the presence of gray hair, people of all ages stood silent, ready to be counseled in the way of wisdom."[2] Things look quite a bit different in our modern circles. Why do our youth programs tend to keep older congregants out? Could it be that we within the youth ministry community have sent a message that we didn't need the wisdom of the aged?

In "From Age Segregation to Intergenerational Community" Eugene Roehlkepartain writes, "The truths, traditions, and values of faith are passed from generation to generation not primarily through programs and curricula, but through meaningful relationships, dialogue and mentoring across generations."[3] Weaved all throughout Scripture we see a command from God to tell the generations of his wonderful deeds. This implies that the older generations were intricately involved in the lives of young people, for the benefit of the entire community. This also implies that the Jewish people were very intergenerational in how they interacted with one another. I believe we'd benefit from pursuing a similar model.

Here are suggestions of how to get some of the wise, aged folks of your church involved in your youth ministry:

- Invite them to be small group leaders.
- Start a card ministry. Ask older congregants to send physical, hand-written cards to your teens.
- Start a prayer ministry. Invite older congregants to partner with teens in your youth ministry and serve as their prayer partners.
- Ask them to help serve snacks. Some of the older ladies in my church setting make amazing desserts! Instead of only asking them to make something, also invite them to serve what they make to the teens.
- Invite older adults to be door greeters or to check teens in each week.

As I became convicted about the need to unite the generations within the body of Christ I took the initiative to start a prayer ministry, matching up forty teens with forty older adults who would commit to praying for one young person in the youth ministry on a daily basis. We held about three fellowship events throughout the year for the adult and teenage prayer partner pairs to spend time together and get to know one another. We played games, ate good food, and just shared life. It was awesome, and let me tell you, it is so much fun watching people in their sixties and seventies compete in "minute to win it" games with teenagers.

All of this benefited the teens, *and* their families, *and* the older congregants of the church. I'll be honest, though: At first, it was pretty awkward for everyone, but because of my deep conviction that we are called to unite the generations, we stuck with it. Around year three I saw a huge shift in the culture of our prayer ministry as the teenagers and adults increasingly enjoyed the relationships they were forming.

Jesus and Intergenerational Relationships

Even Jesus found himself interacting in intergenerational relationships. Although we don't know much about Jesus's childhood, there is one specific story in the gospels where we see Jesus crossing over generational lines to interact with those much older than him, recounted in Luke 2:41-47:

> Every year Jesus' parents went to Jerusalem for the Festival of the Passover. When he was twelve years old, they went up to the festival, according to the custom. After the festival was over, while his parents were returning home, the boy Jesus stayed behind in Jerusalem, but they were unaware of it. Thinking he was in their company, they traveled on for a day. Then they began looking for him among their relatives and friends. When they did not find him, they went back to Jerusalem to look for him. After three days they found him in the temple courts, sitting among the teachers, listening to them and asking them questions. Everyone who heard him was amazed at his understanding and his answers.

There are a few things to note about this account. If you notice, it took Joseph and Mary over twenty-four hours to realize their son was missing. Although this may seem odd to us as Westerners, as we learned in chapter 7, the entire Israelite community felt a responsibility to care for one another. Joseph and Mary simply assumed that Jesus was being watched and cared for by others in their company, because when you're Jewish and living in community, that's just what you do.

Although Jesus wasn't being cared for among their company of travelers as his parents first thought, someone was caring for Jesus in the city of Jerusalem, making sure he had a place to sleep and some food to eat. It's worth noting that when Joseph and Mary found Jesus, he was interacting with others in the temple, forming and fostering intergenerational bonds as they debated the Torah together. This gives light to the reality that intergenerational relationships would have been the norm at that time. Since the Jewish people lived in such deep community, older and younger generations would have interacted together often, as was the case with relationships like that of Samuel and Eli, Naomi and Ruth, and Moses and Joshua.

Bringing Teenagers into the Adult Ministries

As we consider ways to get more older adults involved in youth ministry, we would be wise to find ways to plug teenagers into adult ministries as well. Remember Pastor Brandon and Faith in from chapter 8? Faith is forming relationships with older adults simply by serving on the worship team, and so are the other young people Pastor Brandon is shepherding on his worship team.

Consider approaching some of your church's adult leaders to see how teenagers could be integrated into the adult ministries they oversee.

- Have teens join the tech team at your church.
- Encourage teenagers to be greeters or ushers for Sunday morning services.
- Talk with your senior leadership about having a teenager read Scripture or lead the congregation in prayer on a Sunday morning.
- If there's an older adult group at your church, ask the leader of that group how you and your teenagers could help serve that group.
- Encourage teens who love cooking to join church folks who help provide meals.
- Encourage some of your more mature teens to attend one of the adult mission trips.
- If a teenager has a passion for missions, get them connected with your adult evangelism/outreach team.
- If there is a men's or women's ministry at your church, talk with the coordinators to see if there are any upcoming events, service opportunities, or Bible studies that teenagers could get plugged

into.

- Talk with your children's ministry leader to see if teens can serve alongside adult leaders in leading Sunday school or kids' club.

Whether it's inviting older congregation members to be part of your youth group or looking for ways that teenagers can plug into other ministries, bringing the generations together helps the church grow into the edifice God intended—a beautiful family of loving adults and children.

Let's Not Forget Mom and Dad

As we're discussing the importance of uniting the generations and the church operating as a family, it's essential that we address the reality that the most important factors in a child's faith development are their parents. Since so much time and attention within the youth ministry community have been spent on this topic already, I'm only going to take a small section of this chapter to comment on the family dynamics of faith within the Jewish home.

As Wilson writes, "In Jewish tradition, the center of religious life has always been the home."[4] In fact, after the destruction of the temple in 70 AD, the rabbis started teaching that each home would now act as a temple.[5] Wilson comments, "Just as the *shekhinah* (the abiding presence of God) filled the Temple...so each home was to reflect God's glory through prayer and praise."[6] He also writes, "The dinner table of the home became, as it were, the altar of the Temple...At the table, the father served as priest of his own sanctuary, instructing his family in the words of Torah as one of the priests of old."[7]

The home was the place where the Jewish people put their faith into practice, a living sanctuary reflecting the love of God to those abiding there. Women, not just men, played an important role in the faith development of children within the Jewish home. Each Sabbath the mother was to light the Sabbath candle, inaugurating the beginning of the Sabbath as she spoke the first of the Sabbath blessings over the home.[8] In Scripture we see that it was Eunice and Lois, Timothy's mother and grandmother, who instilled faith in him at a very young age.

Powell, Griffin, and Clark quote a study in *Sticky Faith* that concludes, "Most teenagers and their parents may not realize it, but a lot of research in the sociology of religion suggests that the most important social influence in shaping young people's religious lives is the religious life modeled and taught to them by their parents."[9] This was true in the Jewish home of the first century and it's still true today. Parents matter. If we try to make disciples without them, we'll be fighting an uphill battle.

Family Rhythms for Transformation

Faithful Jewish parents serve as continual reminders to their children to remember the *mitzvot*, or commandments, of God. Devout Jewish families observe the yearly feasts and weekly Sabbath. "The Sabbath is so important that it is looked on as being the primary instrument by which the Jewish people have been sustained and preserved throughout the ages,"[10] Bruce Scott writes in *The Feasts of Israel*. For the Jewish people who observe it, the Sabbath rhythm that's been set in place serves as a continual reminder of their covenant relationship with God and God's goodness and greatness.

Do we have such rhythms built into our own lives? Rhythms that remind us of the greatness of God and of his Word? What takes up the majority of our time on the weekly calendar? Are there any rhythms set in place that bring us into a holy place with God? Consider encouraging families in your youth ministry to start adopting a different rhythm into their calendars by starting some family traditions. Here are some suggestions:

1. Just for fun, try celebrating some of the Jewish feasts.[11]
2. Do family devotions together.
3. Volunteer together.
4. Go on mission trips together.
5. Set aside time each week to simply be still.

6. Have yearly themes for your family—something that calls you each to remember who God is. This could mean focusing on a different Bible character each month or a different book of the Bible each year.

7. Pray for each other.

8. Sing worship songs together at home.

Partnering with parents is essential to making disciples. Youth ministry research supports and encourages youth leaders to see the family, not themselves, as the primary spiritual influencers in young people's lives. Invest in parents. Encourage them to prioritize finding a rhythm that works for their family to incorporate more of God's Word and his greatness into their lives. In the traditional Jewish home the father served as priest and the mother served in teaching her children about God. We should seek to equip parents today to develop spiritual practices and rhythms for their families.

An Extended Spiritual Family

But, what do we do with teens who come into our midst without spiritual roots? Maybe their parents aren't Christians and there's no close relative who's following Jesus either. The Jewish people understood that they were a spiritual family, and we should think of our communities of faith in a similar sense today. Surrounding teens, especially those without spiritual roots or family members who are following Jesus, becomes the responsibility of the community of Christ. As Clark writes,

> When a faith community provides a young person with a welcoming place to belong, a meaningful way to make a difference in their world, and a family that loves and pursues them unconditionally, God's people are responding, in the name of Jesus, to the deepest core needs that a youth can experience.[12]

As Clark goes on to emphasize, it is the church's responsibility to adopt those coming from the outside, bringing them into our family within the body of Christ, acting as spiritual parents, grandparents, and brothers and sisters in Christ.

Francisco's Story

The church becoming a spiritual family was a reality for Francisco, a young man I had the privilege of meeting when I was doing research for my master's thesis. Francisco grew up in a home with no Christian roots. He started attending a local church thanks to a guy who went around town picking kids up for their Wednesday night programming through the church's bus ministry. Francisco told me that over time that little church of seventy people literally became his family. He said that because his family was so broken, church members would have him over for Thanksgiving, buy him Christmas gifts, and pay for him to attend youth retreats and conferences. After he graduated from high school they would check in on him often and send cards in the mail. He told me that without the love, care, and concern of that little church he's not sure he would have continued on in life. He said he refers to many of the little old ladies in the congregation who helped care for him as "Mama." The people of this church believed in Francisco, they invested in him, and they went the extra mile to become a spiritual family for him. In fact, he was serving so much in the church as a teenager that they gave him his very own set of church keys. His youth pastor even started training him up, giving him opportunities to preach at youth group.

This little church understood that their role in the life of a young person went beyond a simple hello on a Sunday morning. They understood they had a responsibility to become Francisco's spiritual family and because of it, Francisco is flourishing in his faith, has graduated from college, and is currently serving as a youth pastor in a local church.

Mark DeVries writes, "It is crucial that young people from nontraditional families feel part of the entire church and not simply a part of the youth program."[13] This is what that little church did for Francisco. Through intergenerational relationships they helped foster faith in one teenager, and it had a lasting impact on his life.

Putting it All Together

As we consider implementing some of what we've learned about the Jewish family, bringing people like Ray into our ministries and becoming a spiritual family for guys like Francisco, we must understand that unless we embrace the calling to connect the generations, we will never actually put these things into practice. Uniting the generations, partnering with parents, and becoming a spiritual family is hard work. However, it is necessary if we're going to follow Rabbi Jesus and the way he did discipleship. There is so much value in seeing the church not as a building or a number of programs but, like the Jewish people of the first century did, as a family.

First-Century Youth Ministry

Just Like Our Rabbi, Jesus

When I was preparing to play on a women's basketball team during my time in Israel, no one told me that there would be a shot clock. In preparation for this trip I'd spent countless hours at the YMCA trying to get in the best physical shape of my life. I did suicides, jumped rope, ran sprints, and did lots of basketball drills. When I was training, the older ladies who were at the Y taking exercise classes would look at me like I was half crazy. But I had a goal in mind, so I kept working hard. I didn't care if that meant I looked foolish. Despite all of my training, though, I was unprepared for how much harder the games would be on me physically with a 35-second shot clock. Discovering I'd have that time restriction was a rude awakening!

Have you ever felt unprepared in ministry? Thinking to yourself, "Gosh, I wish I would have spent more time on _____!"? When it comes to making disciples, we have to take very seriously the need to prepare ourselves well for the task. If we don't, we'll end up like me, huffing and puffing our way down the youth ministry court, wondering when and if the shot clocks of discouragement we face will ever go away.

In the first century, any Jewish person aspiring to become a rabbi would have spent a tremendous amount of time in preparation, getting ready for the task of making disciples. And this would have come at a great cost. Preparing to become a rabbi required nearly every part of a person's intellect, heart, and devotion. However, the task was worth training for, because that training prepared them for what they would face as teachers and leaders of God's people.

Have you prepared yourself well for the task of making disciples, as the Jewish rabbis of Jesus's day did? Have you centered your whole intellect, heart, and devotion on the high calling of investing in people for the glory of God?

The Journey to Becoming a Rabbi

As we looked at earlier, the first-century Jewish educational system was rigorous and challenging. Only a select few, the best of the very best, would continue in their studies to to the point where they'd follow after a rabbi. Only a few of those elite students, whose lives were considered worthy of emulation, would later have the honor of becoming rabbis themselves. The only people called as rabbis were those whose understanding of God's Word was so powerful and whose walks were so set apart that others wanted to know God just like they did.

In Israel, John told us a story about disciples who followed their rabbi so closely that when this rabbi gained a limp through an injury, his disciples emulated that limp as they followed him along the road. Disciples would even follow their rabbi into the restroom, because they wanted to see if he might say a special blessing or prayer. A rabbi's life was so attractive that their disciples wanted to be just like him. Even if it meant following him into the men's room—which I wouldn't recommend you encourage your teens to do!

Normally, a man would have become a rabbi around the age of thirty. It was at this point, after studying under another well-known rabbi through what was called a *yeshiva* (discipleship) experience, that this man was now ready to go and multiply himself by making more *talmidim*. The devotion this took was radical. It meant the aspiring rabbi had to center everything he did around the things of God. It would have literally consumed his life.

It goes without saying that the rabbis in Jesus's day spent a tremendous amount of time in preparation: preparing themselves for the calling of God, centering their lives around the Word of God, and becoming master teachers. Ray Vander Laan says, "Jewish rabbis are widely known for preparing their students well. And Jesus was just like that. He had talked to them. He had demonstrated things to them and he even sent them out."[1] Before Jesus did that, though, he prepared. Jesus spent the first thirty years of his life getting ready. When it comes to ourselves, it can seem much more glamorous to have the title and lead the ministry than it is to continue growing in our understanding of how to be just like our Rabbi Jesus. Yet we cannot ignore the importance of preparation for the rabbis of Jesus's day—and if Jesus himself thought it was valuable to spend many years in preparation, shouldn't we?

In order to prepare our teenagers so that they might go and make their own *talmidim* someday, we must first prepare ourselves. We must be passionately dedicated to this task.

Now That's Dedication

As a first-century rabbi, Jesus would have had the entire Old Testament memorized. This was common for most rabbis in Jesus's day. Can you even begin to imagine how long it would have taken to memorize that much Scripture? The dedication it required would have been absolutely astounding. You would have had to be fueled by true passion and dedication to your calling.

When I think about dedication, I think of the competitors in the Nathan's Hot Dog Eating Contest. The guy who won this past year ate seventy-four hot dogs in ten minutes. That's right, SEVENTY-FOUR HOT DOGS IN TEN MINUTES. My stomach hurts just thinking about it. Honestly, though, that is real dedication. I saw a picture of the winner holding up the prized "Mustard Belt" after his victory. His face said to me, "I did it, now someone please call a doctor."

The people who win these competitions have a passion inside of them and an intense commitment. I mean, it's not like dipping a bun in water actually tastes good. Jesus offers something way better for us to pursue, with results that will be much more lasting—but it will take even more dedication than this past year's winner gave the Nathan's Hot Dog Eating Contest.

You see, even before Jesus became a rabbi, he made a commitment to become a disciple. Yes, Jesus, the son of God, the Word made flesh, was a disciple before he was a disciple-maker. What about us? Are we developing, growing, and maturing, not just as disciple-makers, but as disciples? As David Bivin writes, "Jesus' twelve disciples spent years of intense study and practical training with their master. Later, they themselves were sent out to make disciples and pass on Jesus' teaching."[2] Do we accept the calling to grow as disciples ourselves before we pass on the teachings of our rabbi, Jesus?

You and I must follow Jesus with such devotion that we start to look, act, and think just like him. The only way for us to really know how to make disciples is to first be radically devoted to Jesus himself.

Race Walker

In my home growing up, watching the summer Olympics was a pretty big deal. My sister and I would huddle around the television with Dad, watching the competitions as we cheered for our country. In between some of the bigger events the television network would show quick scenes from Olympic events that don't get as much publicity. One of those happened to be race walking. I was always mesmerized by how fast the athletes' hips could move back and forth. It seemed as though they were flying out of the socket nearly every time they took a stride. I always wondered how people got into a sport like that. I imagined them sitting at the breakfast table one day thinking to themselves, "Well, I don't love running, and just walking is boring, plus that's what everyone else does and I want to be different…so… race walking it is!"

I've never met a race walker, but I can tell you if I did, I'd certainly be able to recognize them by their gait. It's not every day you see a race walker, and their walk would be unforgettable.

For the first-century Jewish people, how a person walked in light of God's commandments was referred to as a person's *halakhah*. Tverberg and Spangler write, "The rabbis' legal decisions for how the Torah should be obeyed were called *halakhah* (halah-KAH), which can be translated 'the path that one walks.' By their rulings, the rabbis were trying to show people how to walk in the way of God's commands."[3]

Covered in His Dust

Jesus had an extraordinary walk. He was so close with God and so in love with God's Word that his walk was unforgettable.

When Jesus stepped onto the scene there were many other teachers already at work, but he was different. What set him apart was the way he understood, lived, and applied God's Word. It wasn't that Jesus had a big gym or a sweet youth room that drew people. It was his walk that made people want to be like him. You and I have been challenged to walk just like our Rabbi Jesus. Why? It's essential for our own sakes, and also because teenagers are looking for something that's real and authentic. They want something they can experience. I often wonder when and if teenagers actually experience Jesus when they come into our youth rooms.

Do you remember in Scripture when Jesus is having a conversation with some religious leaders and they question his desire to heal a man on the Sabbath? Jesus says it's better to heal on the Sabbath, even though many of his contemporaries didn't agree. What motivated Jesus was not legalism, but love. Yes, love was the fuel behind everything Jesus did. Why else would Jesus call the dropouts to follow him? Why would he minister to lepers, care for the outcasts of his society, and love broken, messy people? All of this only happens because his walk was motivated by love.

Let's have an honest moment of reflection together. What fuels our walk? Are we being driven forward by a genuine love for people, a love for God, and a love for his Word, or are we propelled by something else? I don't always like my own answer to that question because more often than I care to admit, I'm not being driven by love. At those times my walk doesn't resemble the walk of Rabbi Jesus, because I don't know or understand him and his love for others and God's Word.

The Mishnah states, "let thy house be a house of meeting for the Sages and sit in the very dust of their feet, and drink in their words with thirst."[4] The phrase "sit at the dust of their feet" comes from the idea that we follow our rabbi so closely that we become covered in their dust. As we follow our Rabbi Jesus, the dust from his feet—feet that traveled down less-than-desirable roads to find the lost, lonely, and hurting—now begins to cover us. And that dust changes us. It can change our youth ministries too. When ministry becomes more about who we can love than what we have to show, we have finally started to understand the way our Rabbi Jesus walked.

Drip, Drip, Drip

In *Walking in the Dust of Rabbi Jesus,* Tverberg writes the story of an old Jewish rabbi and the life-changing power of the Word of God:

> One day as Rabbi Akiva was shepherding his flocks, he noticed a tiny stream trickling down a hillside, dripping over a ledge on its way toward the river below. Below was a massive boulder. Surprisingly, the rock bore a deep impression. The drip, drip, drip of water over the centuries had hollowed away the stone. Akiva commented, "If mere water can do this to hard rock, how much more can God's Word carve a way into my heart of flesh?"[5]

You and I need transformed hearts if we're going to be worthy of making disciples. The most attractive things about our ministries will not be our games, food, or exciting programs. The most attractive things to teenagers are authentic people whose lives are rooted in love, people who are saturated in the life-changing, life-altering Word of God. As the writers of *Growing Young* found, "Honest relationships and the ability to be real or authentic are not only preferences for young people, they also build stronger churches."[6] The more authentic we and our volunteers are, the more attractive and real the gospel becomes to a teenager. The more we invest ourselves into God's Word, the more our hearts start to change. Over time we draw teenagers closer to Jesus not through our style or charisma, but the through the power of God working through us.

Your First Few Steps

Years ago when my nephew was young and learning to walk, he struggled through those first few steps. But oh, they were such glorious steps! With each new day his wobble lessened and his walk became a little sturdier. We have to start somewhere if we're going to pursue God and his Word with radical devotion. It's going to be a little unsteady as we take those first few steps, but, oh, how glorious they are as our lives start to become covered in the dust of Jesus's feet!

Parables: Become a Master Teacher

The rabbis focused their time and attention not just on knowing God's Word but on becoming master teachers of it. The rabbis loved to debate, ask questions, and tell parables. Parables were one of the main ways the rabbis communicated. In fact, over 4,000 parables have survived in rabbinic literature.[7] Jesus himself was a master at telling parables. Through parables master teachers helped bring God's story to life, allowing an opportunity for the listener to insert themselves into it. I learned in Israel that the Bible is a word picture. That's why the Bible is full of symbols like God being our rock and Jesus being the "bread of life," the Pharisees being "whitewashed tombs," and Israel being a vineyard. These were real-life images the rabbis could use to help their listeners better understand the message they were trying to communicate.

I'll be honest: I'm not always operating as a master teacher. In fact, sometimes my teaching has been pretty bad, because, quite frankly, I didn't put as much time and preparation into it as I should have. I've gotten sidetracked and thrown things together quickly. When that's happened the end result has been pretty sad, because my teaching lacks the power of God. On the flip side, there have been times when I have prepared really well, and guess what happens? God shows up! It's in those moments that I see teenagers' hearts captivated. We need more teaching like this. We need more youth leaders who are willing to put the time, energy, and effort into becoming master teachers.

Often, much of what we teach is the sharing of factual information, which we give with the hopes that our listeners will simply agree with what we've said. When teaching on pride we may pull a number of Scriptures that discuss pride, sharing them with our listeners. We'll maybe say something like, "This is what God's Word says about pride, so we should not be prideful. If we're prideful, these are the bad things that might happen. If we're not prideful, here's how our lives will be blessed." There's truth in there, but doesn't that sound boring?

Jesus approached the topic of pride differently. He told this story to a gathering of listeners:

> "Two men went up to the temple to pray, one a Pharisee and the other a tax collector. The Pharisee stood by himself and prayed: 'God, I thank you that I am not like other people—robbers, evildoers, adulterers—or even like this tax collector. I fast twice a week and give a tenth of all I get.' But the tax collector stood at a distance. He would not even look up to heaven, but beat his breast and said, 'God, have mercy on me, a sinner.'
>
> I tell you that this man, rather than the other, went home justified before God. For all those who exalt themselves will be humbled, and those who humble themselves will be exalted."
> (Luke 18:10-14)

This parable about a Pharisee and a tax collector would have completely captured the attention of Jesus's audience. During this time in Israel's history, the Pharisees were thought of by the larger community as the spiritually elite—the group of religious people others should strive to be like. When Jesus says that a Pharisee and a tax collector go up to the temple his listeners would have immediately thought, *Pharisee = good guy, tax collector = bad guy.* The remarkable thing is, Jesus flips it. This would certainly have stunned his listeners because it so subverted their expectations.

While teaching this parable to my youth one Sunday morning, I said to them, "Let's try to think of the most respected Christian occupation—an occupation where others would immediately consider the person in that position as someone to admire and look up to." They chose a pastor. Then, I asked them to think of an occupation that was the lowest of the low, where some people might even hate them for it. They chose a human sex trafficker.

Attempting to take my own shot at coming up with a modern-day parable, our story went a little something like this:

"A pastor and a human sex trafficker go to the front of the altar at church. The pastor prayed, 'God, thank you that I am not like other people, caught in sin and wandering in their faith. Thank you that I have not stumbled like this human sex trafficker or like people who have fallen far from you. I tithe regularly, study the Bible diligently, and pray often for my church congregation.'

The human sex trafficker could not even approach the altar but stood back at a distance, with his head bowed low in shame and guilt. He wept as he cried out, 'God have mercy on me, a sinner!'

I tell you that this man, not the pastor, went home justified before God. Whoever exalts himself will be humbled, but he who humbles himself will be exalted."

As we told our own parable, our youth were drawn in by the real-life example. To them, it now made sense. It was no longer just a story told by Jesus 2,000 years ago, but a real, applicable illustration for their own lives.

It's Time to Hit the Weights

Years ago, I was training for a powerlifting competition. My goal was to be able to lift as much weight as possible. Nearly every day I was hitting the weights, eating right, and then letting my body rest. Over time as I kept practicing, my strength grew.

Your walk, your dedication to your rabbi's teaching, and your devotion to God's Word are what set you apart so that your life might become worthy of emulation. As you continue to live in these things, your faith grows and strengthens, and teenagers will see it. My prayer is that your life will become so attractive that they'll want to know Jesus, just like you do.

It wasn't long after I arrived in Israel years ago that it became overwhelmingly obvious to me that I was ignorant. Ignorant because for the first twenty-five years of my life I had ignored studying the Old Testament. As I sat on a hotel couch in Bethlehem a few days after our journey began, I made the decision to change—to change my devotion to God's Word and start studying all of it, for the first time, with Middle Eastern eyes. Now, years later, something about my relationship with Jesus has radically changed. I have a deeper understanding of his love because of it. Now I long for others to taste and experience God's life-giving Word for their own lives.

As we close this journey together, I am hopeful that you have seen Jesus in a new light and that you are now challenged to go and make your own disciples by becoming just like your rabbi, Jesus. I hope that you would pursue God's Word with radical devotion, seeking to live a life worthy of emulation by immersing yourself in understanding the life, teaching, and ministry of the Lord Jesus Christ. As we seek him, discipleship starts to work, because instead of a program that becomes one more thing for teenagers to have on their to-do lists, we start living radical lives of devotion that others want to copy. We live lives that attract people to the greatest rabbi who ever lived, *Yeshua Ben Yosef* (Jesus, son of Joseph), who left his disciples with one final command: to go and make more *talmidim*, teaching them to obey God's *mitzvot*.

Let's review where we've been together on this dusty road following Rabbi Jesus:

1. The Torah (the Bible) was at the center of Jewish life, teaching, and culture.

2. The community, not the individual, was a primary focus.

3. Jesus practiced a model of "doing life together" in how he did discipleship.

4. To follow a rabbi meant something radical: It meant that you wanted to be just like that person, in every way possible.

5. A rabbi was someone whose life was worth following because of how they loved God and his Word.

6. Discipleship was not a program, it was about learning and doing life together.

7. Mentorship was deeply rooted in the Scriptures and was the means by which ministry was passed on.

8. We should slow down and allow ourselves to enjoy rest with God.

The teens in your ministry need to see the disciples' passion lived out in you. If we are going to make disciples, it has to start with us.

My prayer is that this book has served as a spark from my heart to yours: a spark that has ignited within you a desire to understand Jesus from his Jewish context, a spark to go and make disciples, not for the sake of one more program, but for the kingdom. May we be reminded that the best disciple-maker is someone who is becoming a disciple themselves. May our hearts be lit with the desire to go from key-hoarding leaders to key-sharing leaders. May we run far from pride and toward humility as we commit to the hard work of doing life together, and as we become authentic leaders who share our lives with others for the sake of the kingdom and for this generation of young people. I'm praying for you. I know you can do it.

First-Century Youth Ministry

APPENDIX – An Interview with Jeanne Mayo

I had the privilege of sitting down with Jeanne Mayo in her home on a cool spring day this past year to ask her some personal questions about her own journey of frog-kissing. Remember, frog-kissing is the simple of act of offering a "kiss of encouragement" to help a teenager find their worth and value in Christ. A woman with just over fifty years of experience in youth ministry, who has trained thousands of youth workers across the country and added tremendous value to the youth ministry community, Jeanne is also one of the most kind, caring, and loving people I have ever met. If there's anyone who understands how to create a community where young people feel loved and welcomed, it's Jeanne Mayo.

"Tell me about your journey of frog-kissing and what have been the messiest parts," I said to Jeanne. She said the following:

Gosh, the journey of frog-kissing. It has been the single most important thing I've taught myself to do leadership-wise. I did not grow up in an encouraging home. Many people give themselves a pass on being an encouraging person because they say they're not wired that way. I wasn't wired that way, and it wasn't my personality, and it wasn't the kind of home I grew up in, but I understood the importance of giving people enough emotional energy and hope to be able to be their best possible personal self. I taught myself to verbalize authentic encouragement. Napoleon Bonaparte said, "every true leader is a dispenser of hope."

Well, I think that's what a frog-kisser does. They give hope to people that they're going to be more than they are. They search for what's inside and again dare to keep fanning that, cheering that on, believing in that, until a person gradually transforms into the person God always knew they could be.

Jeanne shared that creating authentic community has been hard and painful.

I think the messiest part is putting my heart out on a stick and having it crushed. You can't deeply believe in people and frog-kiss them without a degree of vulnerability yourself. It's always the people you love the most that hurt you the deepest, so my life is full of stories of people that I've loved deeply, that I've frog-kissed. That I've put my heart out on a stick for and eventually they either trampled my heart or went another way.

In light of all that had been painful, I asked her, "What's made it worth it?" Jeanne said the following:

Oh, I can answer that easily—changed lives. And that sounds so trite and [like] typical religious talk, but it really is the thing that gets me out of the bed in the morning. I think no matter how much money I would ever make in another career field, no matter how "famous" I would ever become in another field, I have the privilege of frog-kissing and believing in some people, and obviously because of the Lord's grace and not my own winsomeness I can totally change the trajectory of their lifestyle.

I asked Jeanne what encouragement she could offer for those of us who want to start doing some frog-kissing of our own. She responded this way:

Whether you do it five minutes a day or an hour in the evening, to believe in people is tremendously non-glamorous. People will rarely appreciate you for it in the moment, but your Christ-centered belief in frog-kissing will be for many, not for all, the game changer in their life… People don't so much celebrate a person who is a hero, but everybody celebrates somebody who makes them a hero.

Endnotes

Chapter 1: Reclaiming Discipleship

1. Marv Wilson, *Our Father Abraham: Jewish Roots of the Christian Faith* (Grand Rapids, MI: William B. Eerdmans Publishing Company and Dayton, OH: Center for Judaic-Christian Studies, 2005), Kindle edition, Ch. 1.

2. Wilson, *Our Father Abraham*, Ch. 1.

3. My Jewish Learning, "Jewish Home and Community," *My Jewish Learning* (website), November 5, 2003, www.myjewishlearning.com/ article/jewish-home-community/ (accessed November 2019).

4. Kara Powell, Jake Mulder, and Brad Griffin, *Growing Young: Six Essential Strategies to Help Young People Discover and Love Your Church* (Grand Rapids, MI: Baker Books, a Division of Baker Publishing Group, 2016), Kindle edition.

5. Chap Clark, *Hurt 2.0: Inside the World of Today's Teenagers* (Grand Rapids, MI: Baker Academic, 2004).

6. Clark, *Hurt 2.0*, Ch.2.

7. Cheryl Hauer, "Discipleship and the Hebraic Worldview," *Bridges for Peace* (website), last modified January 2006, https://www. bridgesforpeace.com/letter/discipleship-and-the-hebraic-worldview/.

Chapter 2: Transformed by the Torah

1. Wilson, *Our Father Abraham*, Ch. 14.

2. Daven: CollinsDictionary.com, *Collins Online English Dictionary*, www. collinsdictionary.com/dictionary/english/daven (accessed November 2019).

3. Ann Spangler and Lois Tverberg, *Sitting at the Feet of Rabbi Jesus: How the Jewishness of Jesus Can Transform Your Life* (Grand Rapids, MI: Zondervan, 2009), Kindle edition, Ch. 2.

4. David Bivin, *New Light on the Difficult Words of Jesus: Insights from His Jewish Context* (Holland, MI: En-Gedi Resource Center, Inc., 2007), Kindle edition, Ch. 1.

5. John Garr, "Lamed—The Tallest Letter." *Bridges for Peace* (website), www.bridgesforpeace.com/letter/lamed-the-tallest-letter/ (accessed November 2019).

6. "Talmud." *Merriam-Webster.com*. 2019. https://www.merriam-webster.

com/dictionary/Talmud (November 2019).

7. Wilson, *Our Father Abraham,* Ch. 14.

8. Ibid.

9. Richard Ross, *Student Ministry and the Supremacy of Christ* (Bloomington, IN: CrossBooks, 2009), Kindle edition, Ch. 5.

10. Garr, "Lamed—The Tallest Letter."

11. Lois Tverberg, *Walking in the Dust of Rabbi Jesus: How the Jewish Words of Jesus Can Change Your Life* (Grand Rapids, MI: Zondervan, 2013), Kindle edition, Ch. 2.

12. Wilson, *Our Father Abraham,* Ch. 3.

Chapter 3: The Disciples' Passion

1. Ray Vander Laan, "To Be a Talmid," *That the World May Know* (website), www.thattheworldmayknow.com/to-be-a-talmid (accessed November 2019).

2. Ibid.

3. Wilson, *Our Father Abraham*, Ch. 14.

4. Garr, "Lamed—The Tallest Letter."

5. Spangler and Tverberg, *Sitting at the Feet of Rabbi Jesus,* Ch. 1.

6. Spangler and Tverberg, *Sitting at the Feet of Rabbi Jesus*, Ch. 2.

Chapter 4: The Keys to the Kingdom

1. Powell, Mulder, and Griffin, *Growing Young,* Ch. 1.

2. Powell, Mulder, and Griffin, *Growing Young,* Ch. 2.

3. *Early Church Video Study: Becoming a Light in the Darkness,* DVD (Grand Rapids, MI: Zondervan, 2015).

4. Powell, Mulder, and Griffin, *Growing Young*, Ch. 2.

5. Ibid.

6. Mark Cannister, *Teenagers Matter: Making Student Ministry a Priority in the Church* (Grand Rapids, MI: Baker Academic, 2013), Kindle edition, Ch. 4.

7. Sara Shendelman and Avram Davis, *Traditions: The Complete Book of Prayers, Rituals and Blessings for Every Jewish Home* (New York: Hyperion, 1998), Part 2.

Chapter 5: Doing Life Together

1. Abigail Wood, "Living in Community," Bridges for Peace (website), June 2015, https://www.bridgesforpeace.com/wp-content/uploads/2015/11/TL_0615_WEB.pdf (accessed November 2019).

2. Ibid.

3. Clark, *Hurt 2.0*, Part 1.

4. Powell, Mulder, and Griffin, *Growing Young*, Ch. 3.

5. Ibid.

6. Kara E. Powell, Brad M. Griffin, and Cheryl A. Crawford, *Sticky Faith, Youth Worker Edition: Practical Ideas to Nurture Long-Term Faith in Teenagers* (Grand Rapids, MI: Zondervan, 2011), Kindle edition, Ch. 7.

7. Andrew Root, *Revisiting Relational Youth Ministry: From a Strategy of Influence to a Theology of Incarnation* (Downers Grove, IL: InterVarsity Press, 2007), Introduction.

8. Powell, Griffin, and Crawford, *Sticky Faith, Youth Worker Edition*, Ch. 2.

9. Root, *Revisiting Relational Youth Ministry*, Ch. 4.

10. Clark, *Hurt 2.0*, Ch. 3.

11. Chap Clark (editor), *Adoptive Youth Ministry: Integrating Emerging Generations into the Family of Faith* (Grand Rapids, MI: Baker Academic, 2016), Introduction.

Chapter 6: Sabbath Rest

1. Ruth Haley Barton, *Sacred Rhythms: Arranging Our Lives For Spiritual Transformation* (Downers Grove, IL: IVP Books, 2006), Kindle edition, Ch. 2.

2. Les Parrott, *Helping the Struggling Adolescent: A Guide to Thirty-six Common Problems for Counselors, Pastors, and Youth Workers* (Grand Rapids, MI: Zondervan, 2000), Kindle edition, Part 2.

3. Clark, *Hurt 2.0*, Ch. 2.

4. Abraham Joshua Heschel, *The Sabbath* (New York: Farrar Straus Giroux, 1951), Part 1, Ch. 1.

5. Ibid.

6. Barton, *Sacred Rhythms*, Ch. 2.

7. Heschel, *The Sabbath*, Part 1, Ch. 1.

8. Ibid.

9. Shendelman and Davis, *Traditions*, Part 2.

10. Bruce Scott, *The Feasts of Israel: Seasons of the Messiah* (Bellmawr: The Friends of Israel Gospel Ministry, Inc. 1997), Ch. 2.

11. Heschel, *The Sabbath,* Introduction.

12. Abraham Joshua Heschel, *Between God and Man: An Interpretation of Judaism* (New York: Free Press Paperbacks, 1959), Ch. 37.

13. R. L. Thomas, *New American Standard Hebrew—Aramaic and Greek dictionaries: Updated Edition* (Anaheim, CA: Foundation Publications, Inc., 1998).

14. Heschel, *The Sabbath,* Part 1, Ch. 1.

Chapter 7: Community-Centered Discipleship

1. Veselin Kesich, "The Church Before Paul," *SVTQ* Vol. 43, No. 1 (1999), 3.

2. Rabbi Jill Jacobs, "The Importance of Community (Kehilla) in Judaism," *My Jewish Learning* (website), https://www.myjewishlearning.com/article/community-focused/ (accessed November 2019).

3. Lois Tverberg, *Reading the Bible with Rabbi Jesus: How a Jewish Perspective Can Transform Your Understanding* (Grand Rapids, MI: Baker Books, 2017), Ch. 7.

4. Jacobs, "The Importance of Community (Kehilla) in Judaism."

5. Spangler and Tverberg, *Sitting at the Feet of Rabbi Jesus,* Ch.10.

6. Barry Jones, "The Dinner Table as a Place of Connection, Brokenness, and Blessing," *DTS Magazine*, October 26, 2015, https://voice.dts.edu/article/a-place-at-the-table-jones-barry/ (accessed November 2019).

7. Dr. Eli Lizorkin-Eyzenberg, "Understanding Jewish Meals in Their Context (by Prof. Peter Shirokov)," May 21, 2014, *Israel Institute of Biblical Studies* (blog), https://blog.israelbiblicalstudies.com/jewish-studies/jewish-meals-in-context/ (accessed November 2019).

8. Ibid.

9. Jeanne Mayo, *Thriving Youth Groups: Secrets for Growing Your Ministry and Creating a Friendship Culture* (Loveland, CO: Group Publishing, 2005), Ch. 1.

10. Powell, Mulder, and Griffin, *Growing Young*, Ch. 5.

11. Ibid.

12. Mayo, *Thriving Youth Groups*, Ch. 1.

13. Ibid.

14. Ibid.

Chapter 8: Kung Fu Discipleship

1. *The Karate Kid*. Directed by Harald Zwart. Beijing. Columbia Pictures, 2010.

2. Root, *Revisiting Relational Youth Ministry*.

3. History Disclosure Team, "Word 'Mentor' Originates from Homer," HistoryDisclosure.com (website), May 4, 2016, http://www. historydisclosure.com/word-mentor-originates-homer/ (Accessed April 16, 2019).

4. Powell, Mulder and Griffin, *Growing Young*, Ch. 5.

5. Jeff Keuss, *Blur: A New Paradigm for Understanding Youth Culture* (Grand Rapids, MI: Zondervan, 2014), Ch. 5.

6. Clark, *Hurt 2.0*, Ch. 1.

7. "Rabbeinu Yonah on Pirkei Avot 1:6," *Sefaria*, https://www.sefaria.org/ Rabbeinu_Yonah_on_Pirkei_Avot.1.6?lang=bi (accessed November 8, 2019).

8. "apprentice." *Merriam-Webster.com*. 2019. https://www.merriam-webster.com/dictionary/apprentice (March 18, 2019).

9. Joshua Moss, "Discipleship, What is It?" *Jews for Jesus* (website), July 1, 1986, https://jewsforjesus.org/publications/newsletter/newsletter-jul-1986/discipleship-what-is-it/ (accessed November 2019).

10. Spangler and Tverberg, *Sitting at the Feet of Rabbi Jesus,* Ch. 4.

11. Ibid.

12. Robert Jamieson, A.R. Fausset, and David Brown, *Commentary Critical and Explanatory on the Whole Bible* (Oak Harbor, WA: Logos Research Systems, Inc., 1997), Vol. 1, p. 227.

13. Alton Chua and Pelham Lessing, "A Biblical Model of Mentoring with a Knowledge Management Perspective," *Conspectus* 15, No. 1 (March 2013) 86-106, https://www.sats.edu.za/userfiles/Chua and Lessing.pdf (accessed April 16, 2019).

14. Ibid.

15. Annita Kerr D'Amico and Rene D. Rochester, *The Culturally-Wired Brain: Why Cultural Bridging is Critical For Learning and Understanding* (Enumclaw, WA: Redemption Press, 2015), Kindle edition, Ch. 7.

16. Spangler and Tverberg, *Sitting at the Feet of Rabbi Jesus*, Ch. 4.

Chapter 9: Church as Family

1. Wilson, *Our Father Abraham,* Ch. 11.

2. Ibid.

3. Eugene C. Roehlkepartain, "From Age Segregation to Intergenerational Community," *Clergy Journal*, Vol. 80, No. 1 (Oct. 2003) 7-9. Academic Search Premier.

4. Wilson, *Our Father Abraham,* Ch. 11.

5. Ibid.

6. Ibid.

7. Ibid.

8. Scott, *The Feasts of Israel*, Ch. 2.

9. Powell, Griffin, and Crawford, *Sticky Faith, Youth Worker Edition,* Ch. 6.

10. Scott, *The Feasts of Israel,* Ch. 2.

11. Jeff Myers, *God Parties: Learning from Feasts and Festivals* (San Diego, CA: The Youth Cartel, 2014), downloadable curriculum.

12. Clark, *Adoptive Youth Ministry,* Ch. 3.

13. Mark DeVries, *Family-Based Youth Ministry* (Downers Grove, IL: InterVarsity Press, 2004).

Chapter 10: Just Like Our Rabbi, Jesus

1. *Early Church Video Study: Becoming a Light in the Darkness.*

2. Bivin, *New Light on the Difficult Words of Jesus*, Part 2, Ch. 1.

3. Spangler and Tverberg, *Sitting at the Feet of Rabbi Jesus*, Ch. 12.

4. "Pirkei Avot 1:4." *Sefaria,* https://sefaria.org/Pirkei_Avot 1.4?lang=bi&with=all&lang2=en (accessed October 25, 2019).

5. Tverberg, *Walking in the Dust of Rabbi Jesus*, Ch. 11.

6. Powell, Mulder, and Griffin, *Growing Young*, Ch. 5.

7. Bivin, *New Light on the Difficult Words of Jesus*, Part 2, Ch. 1.

Made in the USA
San Bernardino, CA
04 January 2020

62658853R00082